Penguin Books
The Calcium Diet

Dr Cedric Garland is the Director of the Epidemiology
Program at the University of California, San Diego Cancer
Center, and an Associate Professor of Epidemiology in the
Department of Community and Family Medicine at the
University of California, San Diego, School of Medicine. He is
a Fellow of the American College of Epidemiology.

Dr Frank Garland is the Head of the Epidemiology Program
and Human Immunodeficiency Virus (HIV) Central Registry
at the Naval Health Research Center in San Diego, California.
He is an Assistant Adjunct Professor of Epidemiology in the
Department of Community and Family Medicine at the
University of California, San Diego, School of Medicine. He is
a member of the American College of Epidemiology.

Ellen Thro, a long-time writer in the fields of health and
environment. She has numerous articles and several books to
her credit. She has received a Distinguished Achievement
Award from the Educational Press Association of America. A
resident of San Diego, California, she has degrees from the
Smith College and the University of Chicago.

Eva Garliano is a graduate of the University of Southern
California and a freelance writer. She lives in La Jolla,
California. She has a special interest in using the findings of
nutritional epidemiology studies to create healthful regional
food recipes.

THE CALCIUM DIET

How to Prevent Osteoporosis,
High Blood Pressure and Cancer

DR CEDRIC GARLAND AND
DR FRANK GARLAND

with Ellen Thro and the assistance of
Eva Garliano

PENGUIN BOOKS

This book is dedicated to Gene and Mary Viola
for their imagination and belief

PENGUIN BOOKS

Published by the Penguin Group
27 Wrights Lane, London W8 5TZ, England
Viking Penguin Inc., 40 West 23rd Street, New York, New York 10010, USA
Penguin Books Australia Ltd, Ringwood, Victoria, Australia
Penguin Books Canada Ltd, 2801 John Street, Markham, Ontario, Canada L3R 1B4
Penguin Books (NZ) Ltd, 182–190 Wairau Road, Auckland 10, New Zealand

Penguin Books Ltd, Registered Offices: Harmondsworth, Middlesex, England

First published in the USA by G. P. Putnam's Sons, New York 1988
Published simultaneously in Canada by General Publishing Co. Ltd, Toronto
Published in Penguin Books 1990
10 9 8 7 6 5 4 3 2

Made and printed in Great Britain by
Richard Clay Ltd, Bungay, Suffolk
Filmset in Monophoto Plantin

CONTENTS

ACKNOWLEDGEMENTS

Many people have helped us with this book. Several gave enormous time and effort in assisting us. Edward D. Gorham, our friend and esteemed colleague, made such a wide range of contributions to the success of the book that it would require a catalogue of activities to list and thank him for each.

There are several individuals who did not take part in writing the book, but whose research work, cited in the book, made many sections possible. Dr Elizabeth Barrett-Connor of the Department of Community and Family Medicine of the University of California, San Diego, was a leading force behind one of the key scientific studies on which parts of this book are based. Dr Michael H. Criqui of the same department arranged an important collaboration and contributed to these studies. Dr Richard B. Shekelle of the Department of Epidemiology of the School of Public Health of the University of Texas Medical Center at Houston generously allowed use of data from a population he and his colleagues had carefully followed. We were then able to collaborate on a study which is described in this book. We greatly value the spirit of scientific cooperation of these friends.

Our students have been a source of help and encouragement. Julia Lynn Vandenburgh assisted greatly during data collection and literature review on some of the studies cited in the book. Medical student Jeffrey Young, who completed a research project on urbanization and mortality rates from breast cancer with us, helped us to recognize and understand why air pollution and urban living are important factors in the risk of fatal breast cancer. Epidemiology student Eddie Ko Shaw helped with the studies reported in this book in a number of ways, particularly with respect to water supplies and air pollution.

A number of specialists across a range of fields generously shared their expertise. These included Wayne Hering, Dr Jerome Namias, and Dr Hans Panofsky of the University of California Scripps Institution of Oceanography, who advised on atmospheric optics and meteorological factors. Dr James N. Pitts Jr of the Statewide Air Pollution Research Center at the University of California at Riverside provided helpful information on the atmospheric chemistry of air pollution. Dr George H. Mount of the National Oceanic and Atmospheric Administration in Boulder, Colorado, calculated the effect of sulphur dioxide on transmission of ultraviolet light, and Dr Arlin Krueger of the National Aeronautical and Space Administration Goddard Space Flight Center provided satellite data from the TOMS instrument on the Nimbus 7 satellite that we used to determine loss of ultraviolet light due to sulphur dioxide air pollution. Dr Joseph Scotto of the National Cancer Institute provided detailed data on ultraviolet light.

The book would not exist if Sandra Dijkstra had not recognized the need for it and brought us together. We owe her thanks. Mr Roger Scholl, our editor, was both incisive and understanding. Numerous colleagues provided information of value, and we thank them for their help. The best qualities of the book are due to those who helped us, but responsibility for the contents is ours alone.

The late Dr Abraham M. Lilienfield of the Department of Epidemiology of the Johns Hopkins University School of Hygiene and Public Health had faith from the earliest days in our belief that ultraviolet light, vitamin D and calcium play a role in reducing risk of breast and intestinal cancers, and we are grateful for his encouragement to nurture the idea.

For the British edition, Linda Edward provided the nutritional details, and Frances Rowe the appropriate data on the environment.

Finally, thanks are due to our families for endless patience and hope.

C.G., F.G., E.T.,
E.G.
La Jolla, California

INTRODUCTION

Our Calcium and Vitamin D Discovery

The Calcium Diet began as a result of our recent news-breaking discovery with colleagues that a diet rich in calcium and vitamin D can help to prevent intestinal cancer. The connections between calcium and osteoporosis, and calcium and high blood pressure have been previously described by other medical scientists. With our discovery of the link between certain types of cancer and calcium, however, we realized, as never before, the essential role calcium plays in our health.

In addition to the critical importance of calcium in the body, we realized that vitamin D plays an important and overlooked auxiliary role. Too often the calcium in the food we eat is unusable. Because of this, health-conscious people may think they are taking in enough calcium according to the various calcium charts and counters currently available, when they are not – because much of what they have taken in cannot be absorbed.

Vitamin D helps the body absorb calcium and plays a major role in the body's ability to use the calcium that is available. An awareness of the role that vitamin D plays in calcium absorption, as well as familiarity with natural calcium 'robbers' (foods that bind calcium and make it unusable) will make an important difference in whether or not you get enough usable calcium daily. *The Calcium Diet* is the first book to bring together all these factors to fashion a complete calcium programme that can be tailored to each individual's needs.

The Calcium–Cancer Link

It has been widely reported that calcium plays a role in osteoporosis and high blood pressure, but our research is the first to link a deficiency of calcium to cancer.

Our discoveries about calcium and vitamin D are grounded in exacting scientific facts – evidence that shows that the risks of breast and intestinal cancer throughout the world vary according to geography. In the United States, generally the farther south people live, the lower the risks of breast and intestinal cancers. People in some northern U S cities have *three times* the risk of dying from these cancers as people in the south. There are even bigger differences in risk among other countries. The question, of course, is why?

Our investigation began on a summer afternoon in 1979. We were sitting in a lecture hall at the Johns Hopkins University, where Cedric was a member of the faculty and Frank a graduate student. We were viewing a presentation of maps of the United States showing the rates of various cancers for each of the 3,056 counties in the United States, information newly computed by Dr T. J. Mason and his colleagues of the National Cancer Institute. On each map, the parts of the country with high rates were darkly coloured, and areas with the lowest rates were white. Most of the maps showed a random, shotgun-like pattern of light and dark. But two maps – one of breast cancer and one of intestinal cancer – struck us with their startling geographic pattern. Although we didn't know it then, we were beginning to unravel an epidemiological mystery.

It looked as if someone had drawn a heavy line along

the thirty-seventh parallel – through the middle of California, and the tops of Arizona, New Mexico, Texas, Tennessee and the Carolinas. Virtually all the places with high mortality from breast and intestinal cancer were north of this line, whereas those with low mortality were south of it. The white low-cancer areas were far more frequent in the sun belt. For example, most of southern California and Arizona were white, as was New Mexico. The dark areas with high mortality were located in the northern half of the country, particularly in the north-east.

Cedric had a flash of inspiration. Could the rates for intestinal and breast cancer be connected somehow with sunlight? Our first step in answering the question was to try to eliminate other possible explanations for the geographic differences. One such possibility involved food. Both fibre-containing vegetables and red meat had been strongly suggested as influences in the occurrence of colon cancer – fibre as a food that helped to *prevent* the disease, and fat and red meat *increasing* its likelihood. Fat had been strongly suggested as a cause of breast cancer, as well. Perhaps eating patterns were different in various parts of the country.

We obtained national dietary consumption patterns from a survey conducted by the American Department of Agriculture. The survey told us that food consumption is remarkably similar throughout the country, including intake of fruits, vegetables, fats and red meat. Supermarkets and fast-food restaurants have standardized eating habits, so geographic differences in food consumption didn't explain the vast differences in intestinal and breast cancer rates across the country.

Our next step was to look at all evidence available to test the theory. We examined patterns of cancer death rates from around the world looking for clues about sunlight and other cancers. One of the first observations we made was that the death rates throughout the world for intestinal and breast cancer were much higher in big cities than in small cities and towns at the same latitude. We guessed that people in big cities at any latitude were deprived of vitamin D as adults due to air pollution and indoor urban lifestyles.

Sunlight, Vitamin D and Calcium

What was the significance of sunlight with regard to cancer rates? Sunlight reacts with cholesterol inside and on the surface of the skin to create vitamin D. Vitamin D helps the body absorb calcium (the correlation between calcium and cancer will be discussed in Chapter 1). Here's how it works:

Three hormones regulate calcium in the body; only one, vitamin D, is to some extent under our control. Vitamin D is the only vitamin that has both a dietary and nondietary source. It is present in a few foods, such as oily fish, but what makes vitamin D so unique is that it's also produced when the skin is exposed to sunlight. Sunshine activates the cholesterol on the skin, creating provitamin-D. A reaction requiring body heat transforms this to vitamin D, which is transported to the liver and kidneys in sequence, where each adds a molecule to it. The final product is transported to the small intestine, where it directs the cells lining the intestine to produce a calcium-binding protein from a part of their DNA, or genetic material. This protein then lies in wait, ready to grab at any unsuspecting calcium coming through the intestine. Once hooked, the calcium is carried everywhere in the body it is needed, including the breast and the rest of the intestine. Without vitamin D, most of the calcium is cast off, completely unused.

Calcium is one of the great binders of nature: it causes cement to harden, blood to clot, bones to hold up. Every cell in the body uses it. It's needed for your nerves to fire, for your brain to function, and for your muscles to contract. Even your heart won't beat without calcium.

What is the relationship between calcium and cancer? Calcium maintains the organization of tissues. Tissues are groups of cells that do the body's work. Coordination among the cells in a tissue is maintained mostly by bridges, known as tight junctions, that bind the cells together physically and allow messages to be carried among them. The messages are carried by calcium atoms just like messages on a telephone line are carried by electrons.

Tight junctions – and communication between cells – disappear when calcium in the fluid around the cells drops. The tissues become disorganized. Competition among the cells for food and oxygen replaces the usual cooperation, and a process of rapid evolution at the cell level begins.

The result of this is that highly specialized, aggressive cells evolve that can command resources, invade other tissues, and kill other cells. This is cancer.

The Western Electric Study

In 1984 an opportunity arose to test the effects of dietary vitamin D and calcium on intestinal cancer in a group of 1,954 men. The men were employed by the Western Electric Company in a telephone assembly plant near Chicago. They were given dietary interviews during 1957–8, and were followed up carefully for occurrence of heart disease and cancer by a distinguished group of scientists, including Drs Richard Shekelle, Arthur Rossof, Oglesby Paul and Jeremiah Stamler.

Our friends and colleagues Drs Michael Criqui and

Elizabeth L. Barrett-Connor of the University of California San Diego Department of Community and Family Medicine met Dr Shekelle at an educational conference on heart disease epidemiology. Both Dr Criqui and Dr Barrett-Connor mentioned our theory to Dr Shekelle, and suggested that it could be tested using the study that Shekelle's group in Chicago had begun years before. Dr Shekelle agreed and we began the analyses.

The study, which we co-authored with Drs Barrett-Connor, Criqui, Shekelle and his colleagues Drs Rossof and Paul, was published in the *Lancet* on 9 February 1985. Dietary histories were collected at the beginning of the study, *before* any disease occurred. The participants cooperated faithfully during the next nineteen years, and all but three of the men remained in the study to the end.

Intestinal cancer takes about twenty years to develop. We know that patterns of intestinal cancer according to foods eaten would be evident because twenty years had passed since the study began. Diet histories for the study had been collected by nutritionists using plastic models to measure precisely the quantities of food eaten during the month before the interviews. The averages of each participant's two histories, one year apart, became the basis of the study. Information on the foods the men ate and their intake of vitamins and other nutrients was calculated and stored for later analysis. At the end of the period, forty-nine of the men had developed colon or rectal cancer and 1,372 men were free of cancer (the rest died of other causes).

We found that men who developed intestinal cancer were a little heavier than those who did not, but they consumed slightly fewer calories than those free of cancer. A typical high-fat intake (43 per cent of the men's calories were from fat) was present in both groups. The two groups ate virtually identical amounts of animal and vegetable protein and carbohydrates. There were no significant differences in intake of saturated or unsaturated fats, dietary cholesterol, minerals (except calcium) and most vitamins. The intake of alcohol differed slightly: heavier drinkers had a slightly higher risk of intestinal cancer.

Much to our excitement, our findings showed that the men who developed intestinal cancer differed from those who did not in only two respects – they ate far fewer foods containing vitamin D and calcium. Men who took in calcium and vitamin D equivalent to four glasses of skimmed milk per day had only about *one third* the risk of intestinal cancer.

The men in the lowest intake group of vitamin D took in about 60 International Units (I U) per day, which is less vitamin D than found in an ordinary glass of skimmed vitamin D-fortified milk (100 I U); whereas the men in the highest intake group took in an average of 336 I U per day, or the amount of vitamin D in three and one third glasses. The men who had the lowest intake of vitamin D developed about twice as much intestinal cancer as those who had the highest intake (Figure 1.1).

There was a threshold effect at 150 I U vitamin D – the amount in one and one half glasses of milk. The study was based on U S A milk which is usually fortified with vitamin D. U S milk contains approximately 1 μg/40 I U vitamin D per 100 ml, compared with U K milk which contains approximately 0.03 μg/1.2 I U per 100 ml. The threshold effect means there was no additional decrease in risk of intestinal cancer for men who consumed more than 150 I U of vitamin D per day.

Figure 1.2 shows the incidence of intestinal cancer according to intake of calcium. Men who took in the lowest amount of calcium (on average about 625 milligrams per day, or the amount of calcium in two glasses of milk) had more than three times as much intestinal cancer as men

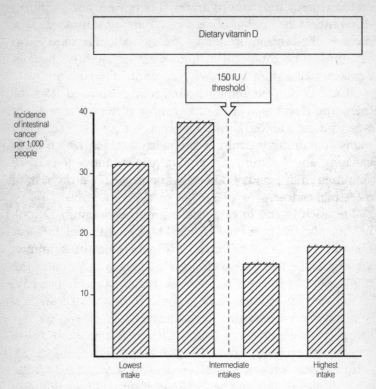

Figure 1.1. Dietary vitamin D intake and incidence of intestinal cancer in 1,954 Western Electric men during 19 years. (*Source:* Garland C., Shekelle R. B., Barrett-Connor E., Criqui M. H., Rossof A. H., Paul O. 'Dietary vitamin D and calcium and risk of colorectal cancer: a 19-year prospective study in men', *Lancet* 1985; 1:307–9.)

who had the highest intake (1,200 or more milligrams per day, or the amount of calcium in four glasses of milk). There was no threshold for the benefit of calcium. This means that we do not know the upper limit of protection that calcium can provide. The more calcium the men took in, the lower the risk they had.

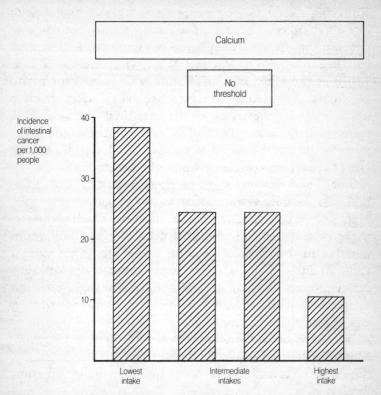

Figure 1.2. Calcium intake and incidence of intestinal cancer in 1,954 Western Electric men during 19 years. (*Source:* Garland C., Shekelle R. B., Barrett-Connor E., Criqui M. H., Rossof A. H., Paul O. 'Dietary vitamin D and calcium and risk of colorectal cancer: a 19-year prospective study in men', *Lancet* 1985; 1:307–9.)

The Laboratory Test

Cedric was invited to the Memorial Sloan-Kettering Cancer Center in New York to present these findings, where the results were warmly received.

Dr Martin Lipkin and Harold Newmark of Sloan-

Kettering were studying people who were at high risk of intestinal cancer because of a strong family tendency to develop the disease. They were pursuing work Newmark had begun with Dr Michael Wargovich and Dr W. R. Bruce at the University of Toronto, Canada. Lipkin and Newmark designed a study to see what effect calcium might have on the tissue of the intestinal tracts of these people. They used a dose of calcium that was about the same as the one we found to be associated with the lowest risk of cancer in our *Lancet* study of Chicago men.

The Sloan-Kettering researchers reported that these high-risk people, before taking calcium, had an unusually high rate of cell division in the intestine. During the test these people took calcium at a dose of 1,250 milligrams per day in the form of calcium carbonate. After two or three months of the dietary supplements, their intestinal cells stopped dividing at the abnormally high rate and adopted a rate of cell division typical of people at ordinary risk of intestinal cancer.

In other words, the clinical test performed at Memorial Sloan-Kettering Cancer Center verified our predictions of the effect of calcium on cancer growth at the microscopic level.

A Curious Exception

There was still one exception to our general findings about the connection between sunlight, calcium and cancer. That exception was one that had been drummed into us by Dr Abraham Lilienfeld at Johns Hopkins. 'Breast cancer is almost nonexistent in Japanese women,' he would say, 'and we have no good explanation. Perhaps someone in this room will discover why.'

Breast and intestinal cancers are most prevalent in places

far from the equator. Most residents of Japan live between 33 and 45 degrees north of the equator, a region with only moderate sunlight. The amount of sunlight reaching Japan is associated almost everywhere else in the world with high rates of breast and intestinal cancer. But the rate of these cancers in Japan is very low – about 5 per 100,000. By comparison, other areas at the same latitude, such as San Francisco and Connecticut, have rates more than five times as high.

We felt that Japan was the odd case, the final telling clue. The meaning of the clue was first discovered two hundred years before, although until our research no one connected the finding with breast cancer. It involved immunity to a disease in Japan that was then causing severely malformed bones in English children. The disease, rickets, was so common in London that it was called the English Disease. It first appeared when people began burning coal on a grand scale in London as early as 1600. As increasing amounts of ash from the coal rose into the atmosphere, the pollution became so bad that it blocked London's sunlight. Before long, everything in the city was coated with grey soot – buildings, trees, even butterflies. In fact, the dark grey butterflies that were appearing everywhere were not just coated with soot – the butterflies were actually emerging from the cocoon dark grey, an early sign of natural selection at work. Light-coloured butterflies were quickly seen by birds against the soot-covered buildings and were eaten. Darker butterflies were blending into the background. In only a few centuries the whole population of butterflies had turned grey.

With urban coal burning and industrialization came bowed legs, knock-knees, and deformities of the chests and pelves of infants and children. The disease became so troublesome that one scientist – a medical explorer – travelled to Japan, where the disease was rare, to find out why. What he found was a population virtually free of rickets, and people who ate a diet loaded with fish.

This aspect of the Japanese diet, which still includes huge amounts of fish, suggested a cure for rickets to that early epidemiologist. It now suggests to us the reason why rates of breast and colon cancer were so low in Japan. Fish is loaded with vitamin D. Although the Japanese do not receive a great deal of sunlight, their *diet* provides the vitamin D their bodies need to help absorb calcium, and prevent breast and colon cancers. This was the missing link, the exception, that confirmed our theories about vitamin D, sunshine, calcium and cancer.

The connection between calcium and cancer had been confirmed. It was but one more way in which we found calcium to be so essential to health. It was at this point that we decided to consolidate our research and the research of so many before us on calcium and its effects, and bring our findings to the general public. More important, given how crucial calcium is to health, we conducted further research to come up with a complete nutritional programme to:

1. determine how much calcium and vitamin D *you* need, and
2. offer a dietary programme to increase the amount of *usable* calcium in your diet.

By following *The Calcium Diet* programme, you can ensure that you are getting enough calcium – usable calcium – to help safeguard against osteoporosis, high blood pressure and cancer. To discover more about the role calcium plays in the body, and how you can increase your calcium intake, read on.

PART ONE

CALCIUM'S ROLE IN THE BODY

CHAPTER ONE

CALCIUM AND YOUR BODY

The human body cannot manufacture calcium. We obtain calcium by eating or drinking foods that contain calcium. On a typical day, the average person takes in about one fortieth of an ounce of calcium, roughly the weight of a small feather (700 milligrams). Unfortunately, usually 15–35 per cent of the calcium we eat is absorbed by the body, depending upon a person's age, sex, vitamin D availability and the presence of other foods that block calcium absorption.

What happens to the calcium that is absorbed? Your body will first allocate the calcium to your blood. If the calcium level in your blood is adequate, it will be shunted quickly to the extracellular fluid around your cells. The extracellular fluid surrounds each cell in your body and gives it the essentials that the cell needs for survival.

Calcium from the extracellular fluid around the cells that make bone will be put to work. You are always making new bone. The process, called remodelling, allows the body to develop new and powerful bones throughout a person's lifetime. The ability to strengthen and develop new bone cells is particularly important for those who are physically active and during pregnancy.

A forty-year-old man taking in an average amount of calcium for his age (700 milligrams) might absorb only 245 milligrams per day. At the same time, his body will lose 100 milligrams of the absorbed calcium in solid waste, 150 milligrams in urine, and 20 milligrams in sweat each day. He will have lost 270 milligrams, but only absorbed 245, leaving him with a daily loss of 25 milligrams.

After a period ranging from minutes to hours, some of the calcium that is absorbed will be used to form a crystal called apatite in the bones throughout the body. It will move fastest to bones which specialize in storing calcium for fast access. These bones, called trabecular bones, are the body's equivalent of a shop which stays open day and night to meet unexpected needs.

Some of the calcium that is absorbed goes to the kidneys, which excrete about 150 milligrams per day. The kidneys conserve calcium; only one hundredth of the amount of calcium that enters them is excreted under normal circumstances, although drinking lots of coffee, for example, can change this ratio, causing the kidneys to excrete much more calcium than they would normally.

Calcium's Job in Your Body

Calcium is used in two ways in your body. The first is for communication. The cells in your body talk constantly, using a special chemical code. They routinely communicate information necessary for your tissues to function properly.

Calcium is vital to that communication between cells. Cells exchange information through tiny bridges between them, called calcium channels. Most calcium channels are located in structures called communicating junctions. Cells transmit various kinds of messages, and we believe that the most important of these is a 'vote' to an adjacent cell on whether to divide.

A normal cell in tissue called epithelium – the cells that

make up the inside layer of your intestine, your skin, and which line the ducts of a woman's breasts – collects 'votes' on whether to divide from adjacent cells, apparently using the calcium channel.

How Calcium Governs Cell Division

Your body can be likened to a giant cooperative venture with billions of cells working towards a common objective, your health.

Many of the most important tissues in your body have an outermost layer that is only one cell thick. This is true of the cells lining the intestine, the cells in the lungs that exchange oxygen and carbon dioxide with the air we breathe, and the cells lining the inside of most of our internal organs. In the case of the small intestine, for example, a single layer of cells is devoted to absorbing nutrients.

What does this mean in terms of calcium and cell communication? Cells communicate by sending molecules from one cell to a neighbouring cell via a communicating junction. When contact between cells is cut off for some reason, we believe that cells interpret this as the loss of a neighbouring cell. The apparent loss of nearby cells seems to stimulate the cells to reproduce. When calcium in the fluid bathing the cells is low, the communicating junction weakens or disappears.

This is the secret of the calcium connection. Calcium is essential to maintaining the system that carries a vital message between the cells that keeps them from dividing unnecessarily. When calcium in the fluid bathing the cells is very low, the communication system is disconnected. The cells can't receive signals from adjacent cells. If enough time passes without receiving signals from adjacent cells, the cells that make new epithelium will divide. If the two cells produced do not receive signals from other cells, they too will divide. If the four cells produced by their division do not receive signals via communicating junctions from other cells, they too will divide, producing eight cells, and so on.

Before long, there will be several generations of new cells, each generation doubling the size of the previous generation. If these cells do not continue to receive growth-blocking signals via communicating junctions from adjacent cells, they will continue to proliferate in a chain reaction. Soon the cells will form a pile-up, and take on peculiar shapes and sizes. When the pile-up is large, the condition is called hyperplasia.

Hyperplasia may be physical evidence of the breakdown in communication among cells. In the intestine, it appears long before cancer is present. A common indication of a breakdown in communication in the cells of the intestine may be for the cells to pile up until they form a polyp, which is an unusual extension of the lining of the intestine into the lumen, or opening, where the food passes through. The cells are limited in how far they can expand back into the tissue, so eventually there isn't anywhere for them to go except out into the lumen.

If you look at polyps under a microscope you will see that many are disorganized tissues. Most polyps don't start out as cancer, but rather seem to be a result of the body's attempt to deal with epithelial cells that are needlessly dividing due to a deficiency of calcium in the fluid bathing them.

Calcium, Cell Division and Cancer

This function of calcium has opened up a new window on

the way cancer works. It may be the missing piece in a puzzle that has bedevilled scientists since the earliest days of cancer research.

Cancer, we think, happens in three phases: decoupling, initiation and promotion. It is during the first phase, which we call decoupling, that calcium has the greatest effect.

Decoupling

Decoupling is the process of cells splitting apart from one another. It happens when the amount of calcium in the extracellular fluid is low. It is due to loss of tight junctions that bind together cells of the intestine, breast and some other tissues. As we discussed above, cells in many tissues will divide unless they receive a signal from neighbouring cells. If that signal is blocked, as by a piece of plastic film between the cells, then cells on both sides of the film divide.

Most cells in your body are constantly taking 'votes' on the question of whether or not to divide. Calcium allows the 'votes' to be communicated. Certain molecules pass easily from cell to cell, like electrons in an electrical wire, but only when the cells are in close contact and calcium is present. If for any reason the flow of molecules between cells is interrupted, the signal cannot be transmitted, and the cells that make new epithelium will begin to proliferate. It would be as if you had cut an important wire in an electrical circuit. The signal cannot be transmitted, and the cells that make new epithelium will proliferate.

When cells lose communication and begin to divide on their own, the tissue becomes disorganized and the cells begin to pile up. This chaotic mitosis or cell division, resulting in large crowds of cells, is called hyperplasia. If the cells are unusual shapes or are especially disorganized, it is called dysplasia. It isn't cancer, however – it often disappears spontaneously without a trace. Decoupling lays the groundwork for hyperplasia and dysplasia, which may precede the next stage in the formation of cancer, initiation.

Initiation

We think three of the primary requirements for cancer are decoupling, induced genetic variation and rapid turnover of cells. Radiation or toxic chemicals can produce genetic variation by attacking the DNA in the cells, causing mutations. Most of the mutated cells will die but a few will thrive. Those that thrive are better able to get food and oxygen than normal cells and therefore better able to reproduce.

If a generator of variation continues to act – if, for example, X-rays are continually applied or chemical carcinogens are continuously present – more variation will occur. New mutations will arise in each generation of transformed cells. Again, most will die but those that thrive will do so because they have an advantage in getting food and oxygen. These cells in turn will thrive and reproduce. Those that reproduce most rapidly are the most successful. If this process continues over many generations, a generation of highly aggressive, rapidly reproducing, mutated cells will come into being. These cells become potent competitors for food and oxygen at the expense of normal cells. In many cases they lose their fine structure and even some of their genes. These are cancer cells.

If the generator of variation is removed, such as removing the carcinogen, or eliminating the radiation, the evolutionary process may be arrested before a new generation of cancer cells evolves. This is probably what happens, for example, when a person stops smoking. The predominant carcinogen in tobacco smoke is benzo-alpha-pyrene. Take it away and evolution of the cells towards cancer is usually arrested.

Sometimes the rescue may come too late. If the cancer cells have evolved sufficiently already, then taking away the generator of variation, or tobacco smoke, will do little good. The die has been cast. This is why stopping smoking late in life doesn't always prevent cancer.

Promotion

The third stage of cancer is proliferation of the highly evolved cancer cells. A cancer can be *promoted* by a chemical that is not a cause of variation. There are many chemicals, such as the hormone oestrogen, that do not appear to initiate cancer cells, but which can stimulate them to grow. This is very practical information since it tells us we can arrest or retard the growth of cancers if we take away any promoters present. The rate of spread of breast cancer can be reduced in many women, for example, by eliminating hormonal promoters. This can be done with a medicine known as tamoxifen, which is a hormone blocker. Without the promoter, the cancer tissue slows its rate of reproduction. Unfortunately, it doesn't stop reproduction completely, so eliminating promoters does not cure cancer. But it can extend life.

How Calcium Prevents Intestinal Cancer

Calcium acts to prevent intestinal cancer in the decoupling phase of the disease.

When calcium levels drop in the fluid that bathes the cells, the tight junctions between the cells disappear. The reason why they vanish is unknown, but their disappearance seems to be a self-protective mechanism intended to tide the cells over until the calcium level in the fluid bathing them rises.

It has an unfortunate side effect. It cuts off close contact with nearby cells. Cells can function normally without communication with other cells, at least for short periods of time. Eventually, though, this isolation will allow the cells to divide. On the other hand, if calcium levels remain normal, cells will not divide unnecessarily, and the evolution towards cancer that can result from abnormally rapid cell division will be slowed. A sufficient intake of calcium slows the evolution of normal cells towards cancer and can help to *prevent* it.

Calcium and Structure

The second major role of calcium in the body is to provide structure. There are only a few elements in the world that are used routinely to provide structure for plants and animals. Almost all rigid structures of plants and animals contain calcium. Each cell in your body, with a few exceptions, has a skeleton, called a cytoskeleton, which keeps the cell together. These cell skeletons differ in degree of rigidity, but in places where they must be very rigid they include crystals of calcium. The reasons for this are that calcium is strong, easily dissolvable and transportable.

Your Bones

The same qualities that make calcium so expedient as a skeleton for the cells – its ability to be dissolved readily and moved from place to place – make it essential for strong bones as well. The disease osteoporosis, in fact, occurs because calcium is easily dissolvable and transportable. A more complete discussion of osteoporosis occurs in Chapter 3.

How are bones formed? In the months preceding birth,

collagen, a tough substance used by the body where flexible strength is needed, forms a net where bone will be created. Calcium in the fetus is then carried from the placenta to this net, where the calcium crystals are neatly caught from one edge of the developing bone to the other. In the months and years that follow, more calcium is added to the bone structure, giving the bone strength.

Calcium is essential to the body at the cellular level, as a structural support and as a means of communication between cells, and in the formation and endurance of bones as well. Because of its importance throughout the body in a variety of functions, a sufficient calcium intake is crucial to health and fitness.

CHAPTER TWO

CALCIUM AND CANCER

Breast Cancer

Breast cancer is one of the most common cancers in women, and among the most deadly. Worldwide, more women die of breast cancer than any other form of cancer. The incidence rate has been increasing steadily. There are about 21,350 new diagnoses and more than 13,500 deaths from breast cancer in England and Wales each year. We believe most of these deaths can be prevented.

The risk of breast cancer is highest in areas that receive low levels of sunlight (Figure 2.1). Because of this we studied the effects of sunlight on mortality rates of breast cancer in the United States.

The U S National Oceanic and Atmospheric Administration reports on sunlight striking the ground at a series of points throughout the country. With medical student Jeffrey Young, we located twenty-nine major cities and fifty-five areas where both data on sunlight and mortality rates were available. The data were specific for size of the population, age and race.

With the help of fellow epidemiologist and friend Edward Gorham, we constructed a graph of the average daily sunlight versus the rate of fatal breast cancer for the major U S cities (Figure 2.2).

As we expected, the *more* sunlight a city received, the *less* was the mortality from breast cancer. As you can see,

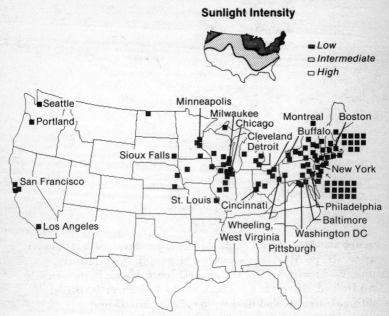

Figure 2.1. Breast cancer hot spots and sunlight intensity.
Source: **American National Cancer Institute.**

the lowest rates were in Honolulu, Phoenix, Albuquerque, Las Vegas and El Paso. These cities received the highest amounts of sunlight of any cities in the United States (all in excess of 500 calories per square centimetre of land area per day).

The highest rates were in New York, Washington, D C, Chicago, Cleveland and Boston. These are all cities that received much less sunlight (250–365 calories per square centimetre per day).

You will notice that New York, Washington, D C, Cleveland, Columbus, Los Angeles and San Diego are all well above the line. They all have more breast cancer than

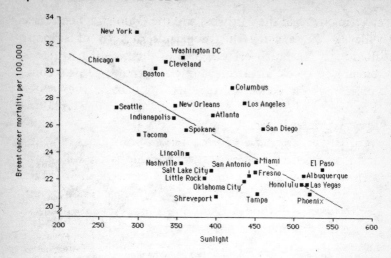

Figure 2.2. As sunlight levels increase, incidence of fatal breast cancer drops. Mortality rates are highest in the relatively sunlight-deprived cities of the north-east, lowest in the sunbelt and Hawaii. *Sources:* **American National Cancer Institute, National Oceanic and Atmospheric Administration.**

expected based on average sunlight level alone. This points to an important factor in the sunlight equation: air pollution. These cities *all* suffer from some form of air pollution. Certain types of air pollution selectively block out a part of the range of ultraviolet light known as UV-B, the part of the sunlight spectrum (295–310 nanometres) that creates vitamin D in the skin and that causes sunburn. The result is that it is hard to get enough vitamin D from the sun in cities with significant air pollution.

The worst blockers of ultraviolet light among ordinary air pollutants are sulphur dioxide and its atmospheric aerosols. This is the air pollution that results from burning coal with high sulphur content in commercial power plants and industries. Much of this coal is burned for cheap electric power in the Midwest and the Ohio and Tennessee valleys. Winds carry the thousands of tons of sulphur dioxide to the north-eastern part of the country, where it remains to block ultraviolet light and create aerosol compounds which reflect ultraviolet light back into space (Figure 2.3). Aerosols are suspensions of fine solid or liquid particles in air.

In Britain, around 70 per cent of sulphur dioxide pollution is emitted by power stations and industry. Emissions declined significantly from the 1960s to reach their lowest level in 1984–5, although they have since risen again. Highest concentrations of sulphur dioxide occur in Yorkshire and Humberside and the East Midlands – where some of the largest coal-fired power stations are located – and Greater London. Some of Britain's sulphur pollution is blown to Scandinavia on north-westerly winds and the Government has initiated a programme to cut sulphur dioxide emissions from several of its larger power stations. Sulphur dioxide is nevertheless still a significant pollutant.

Less effective in removing ultraviolet light, but still of importance, is the air pollution found primarily in the south-western part of the US, smog. Smog occurs when sunlight reacts with the exhaust from cars and pollutants from commercial power plants and industries (particularly nitrogen oxides) depleting ultraviolet light before it reaches the ground.

While smog is not yet such a significant air pollution problem in Britain, scientists predict an increase in California-style smog, especially in southern England.

When we recently uncovered evidence of the powerful blocking effect of sulphur dioxide at the wavelength needed to make vitamin D, we added this factor to our analyses. When we did this, cities that were once above

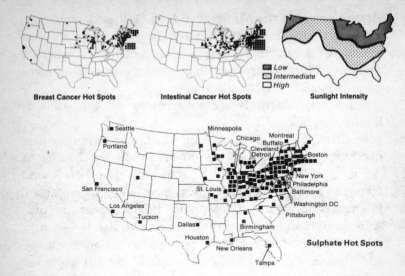

Figure 2.3. Mortality from breast and intestinal cancers is highest in areas with high concentrations of airborne sulphate particles, sulphate 'hot spots'. *Sources:* **Ambient concentrations of sulphur dioxide in the optical path were calculated from data provided by the American Environmental Protection Agency and other reporting sources.**

the diagonal prediction line (Figure 2.2) moved closer to a recomputed diagonal line (Figure 2.4). With these factors it is possible to explain 72 per cent of the geographic variation in the occurrence of fatal breast cancer.

The impact of air pollution in major cities is magnified by urban lifestyles. Forty per cent of those who live in England and Wales inhabit cities, and urban dwellers spend the majority of their lives indoors. On weekdays, most people's brief exposure to the sun on the way to and

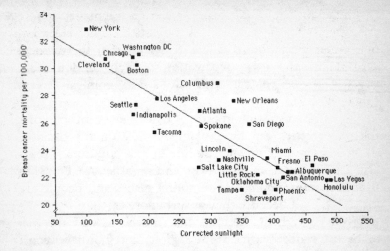

Figure 2.4. The drop in rates of fatal breast cancer with increasing sunlight becomes clearer when the measure of sunlight is adjusted ('corrected') for air pollution from sulphur dioxide and ozone. Los Angeles, New York and several other cities with serious air pollution have moved closer to the diagonal line (compare with Figure 2.2) suggesting that sunlight is a better predictor of mortality rates when adjusted for the pollutants that block ultraviolet light. *Sources:* **Calculated from data provided by the American National Cancer Institute and the National Oceanic and Atmospheric Administration.**

from work occurs when little UV-B from the sun is present.

Urban architecture also cuts our exposure to sunlight. For example, the concrete canyons between the skyscrapers of Manhattan, New York, receive only tiny amounts of sunlight, blocking 95 per cent of rays to the street below. Even a row of ten-storey London buildings, small in comparison, will delete virtually all sunlight from the city's streets. This may help to explain why Manhattan has the highest rate of fatal breast cancer on the planet. There are other factors to consider as well, such as the relocation of women with breast cancer to Manhattan for medical care. None the less, deprivation of light undoubtedly plays a major role in this city's astronomical breast cancer rate.

Most of the variation in rates of fatal breast cancer among the major cities can be explained solely on the basis of differences in sunlight and sulphur dioxide pollution. This is also true in small cities, towns and rural areas. The skin produces more vitamin D in sunny places and people are protected by it because they absorb more calcium.

While sunlight is the clue that showed us why the risk of breast cancer varies from region to region, we don't advise that you spend more time in the sun, as overexposure to UV-B is a major cause of skin cancer. Instead, we recommend that you follow the dietary guidelines for the Calcium Diet presented later in the book.

A Closer Look at the Relationship Between Air Pollution, Light and Cancer

After a few days in the air, sulphur dioxide converts to aerosols of sulphuric acid and ammonium sulphate, and remains for days to weeks strongly reflecting UV-B back into space. The people living in areas with high pollution from sulphur dioxide and its aerosols cannot produce vitamin D in their skin except during two or three months a year. Like many people, they get so little vitamin D from their diet and sunlight that they are seriously deficient in it.

Take a careful look again at Figure 2.3. The figure shows sulphate air pollution, a product of the oxidation of sulphur dioxide. The inserts show maps of hot spots of fatal breast cancer, intestinal cancer and sunlight intensity.

When you first glance at the maps you can see the relationship. The reason is that the areas with high sulphate pollution levels also have high rates of breast and intestinal cancer.

Sulphur dioxide and sulphate pollution filter out the part of ultraviolet light that creates vitamin D. It is the lack of vitamin D that results in the increased incidence of fatal breast and intestinal cancer.

The more sulphur dioxide, the less ultraviolet light, and the more you will need to supplement your diet with vitamin D and calcium, up to the amounts we recommend on pages 85–6. Sulphur compounds in the atmosphere play a major role in predicting the risk of vitamin D deficiency diseases.

Seattle has low pollution from sulphur dioxide and its aerosols and also low rates of breast and intestinal cancer, considering its latitude. Westerly winds may blow Seattle's sulphur dioxide away from the city before most aerosols form. New York has the highest levels of sulphur dioxide aerosol pollution. The rate of fatal breast cancer in New York is nearly double that of Seattle, and the rate of fatal intestinal cancer in New York is also much higher.

Aerosols created by sulphur dioxide create a diamond-like sheen that reflects the sun's brilliant ultraviolet light back to space over New York and the north-east leaving a shadow nearly devoid of the ultraviolet wavelength that creates vitamin D. Add to these particles of soot and dirt in the atmosphere from industry, and you have a curtain of darkness covering the north-eastern United States and parts of Canada. The sulphur dioxide and nitrogen oxides in the atmosphere also cause acid rain and acid fog.

New Hampshire and Maine are hundreds of miles from

major industrial centres, and the rural lifestyle outside the main cities in these areas would normally be expected to be healthy. The reverse is true. Beautiful rural New Hampshire and Maine, two of the most pastoral places in the United States, have higher death rates from breast cancer than forty-six other states, including the most teeming, heavily industrialized states. The rate is shockingly high in all of New York State, too – and the rate in the province of Quebec is higher than in any other part of Canada. The same is true for death rates from intestinal cancer. We believe these high cancer death rates are due primarily to the curtain of darkness from sulphur dioxide and its aerosols carried east by winds from power and industrial plants.

Worse, when breast and intestinal cancers strike in these regions, they are more likely to kill than in the sunny south-west or in the Pacific north-west.

Ozone

Most of the ultraviolet light coming from the sun, about 99 per cent, is filtered out by the Hartley Band of ozone, which is thickest about fifteen miles high. The band has existed for millions of years and protects us from dangerously high levels of ultraviolet light. Ozone concentrations drop off at five miles above the surface, and increase again at ground level, due to local air pollution.

A key example of ground-level ozone pollution occurs in Los Angeles, where ozone levels become very high during the morning and afternoon rush hours. The photochemical reaction that produces ozone removes large portions of ultraviolet light.

UK ground-level ozone shows wide variation. London

records the highest concentration, clustered around the summer months June to September. Ozone levels in rural areas also have a summertime peak as cars take to the roads during the main holiday season. Ozone levels have been known to reach or exceed levels at which human and plant health may be endangered, according to World Health Organization guidelines.

Fish, Vitamin D and Cancer

Japan is at about the same latitude as San Francisco and receives about the same amount of sunlight, but as we discussed in the introduction, the rates of breast cancer are astronomical in San Francisco and very low in Japan. The reason for this, we believe, is the enormous amount of fish consumed daily in Japan, a food rich in vitamin D. The Japanese have for centuries consumed six times the US recommended daily allowance of vitamin D. Very few people in North America or the UK consume anything like this amount.

Women who migrate from Japan to California have a radical increase in rates of fatal breast cancer. The rate in one area of Japan is 5 per 100,000 women per year; it rises to 29 per 100,000 per year in Japanese women who move to the United States. The reason for this is that the food the women eat changes dramatically with the move – Japanese women who have moved to California from Japan and who have taken on a US diet consume one twentieth as much vitamin D as their relatives in Japan. Perhaps it's no surprise that Japanese women here have a higher incidence of breast cancer.

Many fish that are popular in Japan contain very high amounts of vitamin D. Salmon, a favoured item, contains

500 or more I U of vitamin D per 3.5-ounce serving. A popular sushi bar speciality, Anago (eel), is the richest natural source of vitamin D in the world. A 3.5-ounce portion contains 5,000 I U of vitamin D.

The typical woman outside Japan consumes less than a fifth of the vitamin D she needs. Women from the U K, Eire, the United States, Canada and New Zealand are at extremely high risk of fatal breast cancer. These are areas of relatively little ultraviolet light and extremely low intake of dietary vitamin D. In Central America or Africa, by contrast, where bright light is abundant, women have extremely low rates of breast cancer.

The Baby Bonus

Women who have had children in parts of the world where vitamin D levels are high have a lower risk of breast cancer than childless women in the same areas. During pregnancy, vitamin D receptors appear in the tissues of the breast. These are molecules that help the breasts to absorb vitamin D. The breasts in turn absorb more calcium. The purpose is to produce milk. The high level of vitamin D present in the breasts during pregnancy and the absorption of calcium which it stimulates seem to cut the risk of the first stage of cancer. The benefit appears thirty to thirty-five years later as a flat blip in the climb of cancer incidence rates with age. We call this blip the *pregnancy plateau*.

Epidemiological studies of women in Japan, where intake of vitamin D is high, show a strong pregnancy plateau for breast cancer. Countries that have intermediate levels of vitamin D tend to have less evident plateaus and intermediate levels of protection associated with having babies. Countries such as the United States, Canada and most of Europe, however, where vitamin D levels are low, show virtually no pregnancy plateau.

Fat and Cancer

Contrary to widespread opinion, fat does not directly cause breast cancer. A number of years ago researchers observed an apparent correlation between fat consumption in various countries and risk of breast cancer. But a recent long-term study of more than 89,000 nurses by Dr Walter Willet and his colleagues of Harvard University showed that the risk of breast cancer is unrelated to intake of fat in the usual dietary range in North America, the UK, Eire and most industrialized countries (30–40 per cent of total calories).

Dietary fat can bind calcium, however, making it less absorbable. We believe that people who have a diet very high in fat may become deficient in absorbable calcium. Because of fat's ability to bind calcium, women with a high-fat and low-calcium diet could be at even higher risk of breast cancer than women who have only a diet low in calcium. We recommend that women cut fat intake to 20 per cent of total calories to assure adequate calcium absorption. This level of fat intake will also reduce risk of heart disease.

Intestinal Cancer

The three leading causes of cancer death in the UK and United States are lung, intestinal (colorectal) and breast cancers. In England and Wales in 1987 there were 11,380 deaths from colon cancer and a further 5,675 from cancer of the rectum. You've just learned how to minimize your chance of getting breast cancer. If you're a male, there is no need to worry about getting breast cancer (only a small proportion of men are diagnosed with it each year). The best answer to preventing lung cancer has been long established by epidemiologists – avoid smoking tobacco. By following the guidelines in this book you may be able to cut your risk of intestinal cancer by two thirds, as well.

As with breast cancer rates in America, the rates of intestinal cancer are significantly higher in the north than in the south. Within the high-rate area there are 'hot spots', places where the rate is even higher. The leading cities in intestinal cancer hot spots in the continental United States are shown in Figure 2.5. The hot spots are based on reports of death rates for white females from the American National Cancer Institute. Hot spots for intestinal cancer in men are virtually identical to those for women and therefore are not shown. Each hot spot has a mortality rate from cancer of the large intestine that is significantly higher than the US average for white females. The rates have been adjusted for age differences among cities, so the rate is not explained by the differences in the ages of the people who live there. Nor is it due to differences in race among the areas, since these maps show rates only for whites (maps for other races are available in publications of the American National Cancer Institute).

The small map inset on Figure 2.5 shows sunlight levels. The areas outlined in solid black, including New York, Chicago, Boston, Philadelphia, New Haven, Pittsburgh, and Cleveland, receive the least sunlight of any of the 29 major cities in the United States, less than 365 calories per square centimetre per day. Montreal, Canada,

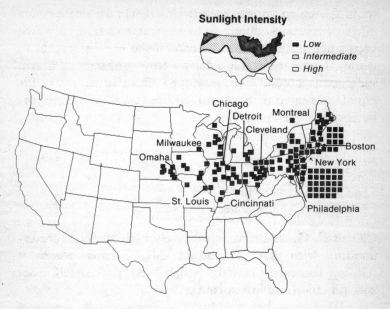

Sunlight Intensity

■ Low
▫ Intermediate
□ High

Chicago
Detroit   Montreal
Cleveland
Milwaukee
Omaha   Boston
New York
St. Louis   Cincinnati
Philadelphia

Figure 2.5. Fatal intestinal cancer, like breast cancer, hits hardest in areas with the least sunlight. This map shows countries with significantly high rates of cancer of the large intestine (colon). Counties with low sunlight levels (upper right) are the most affected. *Sources:* **American National Cancer Institute, National Oceanic and Atmospheric Administration.**

receives 300 calories. All hot spots for intestinal cancer are in or near the low-sunlight zone.

There are no hot spots in the high-sunlight zone. This zone has many areas where rates are significantly *lower* than the US average. These include most counties in California's sunny San Joaquin Valley; Tucson and Phoenix, Arizona; Albuquerque, New Mexico; El Paso, Texas; and Miami, Jacksonville, Tampa, and Orlando, Florida.

Latitude and the concentration of smoke in the air appear to be two significant factors influencing the hot spots for colon cancer in Britain, which is located in a range of latitudes, about 50 to 58 degrees north, in which even small differences in latitude make big differences in winter. Compare average daily figures of hours of bright sunshine (recorded February 1988) from Inverness in the Highland region of Scotland, to the Isle of Wight, in the far south of the country.

Inverness	1.82 hours
Newcastle	3.67 hours
Coventry	3.62 hours
London	4.00 hours
Isle of Wight	4.76 hours

Overall, Great Britain's relatively high latitude (corresponding with that of Hudson Bay, Canada) means it receives less ultraviolet light than New York, itself a hot spot for colon and breast cancer.

Coal burnt as domestic fuel has been the main source of smoke in the UK in the past, the fine particles in the air contributing to the infamous pea souper fogs of the 1950s which proved fatal to numbers of city dwellers. Since the 1960s, however, smoke levels have been reduced partly due to the introduction of the Clean Air Acts which encouraged consumers to switch from coal to smokeless fuels, gas or electricity.

The largest concentrations of smoke today occur in Yorkshire and Humberside, Northern Ireland and the Midlands.

The world over, intestinal cancer predominates in areas with little sunlight, either from weather or air pollution. The highest-risk areas in the world are: Birmingham, New York City, most of Germany, the state of Connecticut, Warsaw, New Zealand, Denmark, Sweden, Leningrad, Moscow and Montreal. The lowest-risk are: Ibadan, Dakar, Honduras, Nicaragua, Chile, Sicily and

Japan. All high-risk areas receive less than 400 calories per day of sunlight per square centimetre of ground. All low-risk areas except Japan (whose people consume much larger amounts of dietary vitamin D) receive more.

How Much Calcium and Vitamin D is Enough?

The point behind all these studies is to show that the amount of sunlight, and therefore vitamin D, a person receives varies according to geography and local conditions. People who receive a great deal of sunlight need *less* dietary vitamin D, because their bodies produce more vitamin D from the sun than people from low-UV-B areas. People in the north and in heavily polluted regions need *more* calcium and vitamin D because of the lack of sufficient vitamin-D-producing sunlight.

People living in Great Britain, a high-latitude country which receives low levels of ultraviolet light, should assume that they will need more calcium and vitamin D than those living in lower latitudes. Exactly how much calcium and vitamin D a person needs will vary.

The present recommended daily intake of vitamin D in most countries is 200 to 400 IU per day. Vitamin D is available from salmon and some other kinds of fish, as shown in Chapter 8. It is also available in some foods to which it has been added. You can find the amount of calcium and vitamin D you need from the charts listed in the same chapter.

We don't recommend increasing the amount of sunlight you receive by exposing yourself for longer periods of time to direct sunlight. People who live in northern climates are usually not well adapted to strong sunlight, and run a considerable chance of developing skin cancer due to overexposure. For this reason we suggest moderate or little intentional direct exposure to the sun, particularly from 10 a.m. to 2 p.m. The same wavelength of light that stimulates production of vitamin D in the skin, UV-B, increases the risk of skin cancer.

CHAPTER THREE

CALCIUM AND OSTEOPOROSIS

As we discussed earlier, in Chapter 1, your body cannot make calcium. The only way your body can obtain it is by eating or drinking foods that contain it. As we explained, your body needs calcium for a variety of reasons, particularly on the cellular level. If it does not obtain enough calcium from the foods you eat, your body's first tendency is to sacrifice calcium from its only reservoir – your bones – to provide calcium for those functions for which it is even more crucial. Ninety-nine per cent of the calcium in the human body is stored in bones. When calcium in other parts of the body runs critically short, calcium from the bones is dissolved and carried away to those parts of the body that need it more. If the body goes for a long period of time with a calcium deficit, the bones can become extremely porous and brittle, resulting in osteomalacia, a loss of mineral from bone. This can lead to osteoporosis.

The loss of calcium from the bones starts with the hip bones, the head of the large leg bones, and the vertebrae, or spinal bones, which are the bones where calcium is stored for rapid access in time of need. People who have a calcium-deficient diet may sacrifice small amounts of calcium from their bones for years without knowing it, until the bones break.

Keeping your bones strong and healthy is a lifelong proposition. Osteoporosis is not something you can overcome simply by ingesting more calcium after the fact. You cannot make up for years of calcium depletion in the bones by overloading your diet with calcium. The key to preventing or retarding osteoporosis is making sure that your body receives a sufficient amount of calcium day after day. You need to start a proper calcium programme *today*, whether you are eighteen or eighty. We will tell you how to set up a proper calcium programme in the chapters that follow.

Calcium Deficiency

In order for calcium to be used by your body, it must be absorbable. Most of the calcium your body takes in is not absorbed. Therefore it is important to distinguish between calcium and *usable* calcium – calcium that can be used by your body. If you are an adult, you will need to take in 800 to 1,200 milligrams of calcium per day (see chart on page 85) for your body to absorb enough calcium to prevent osteoporosis, as well as other diseases resulting from an insufficiency of calcium.

Most adult women and many men lose calcium every day of their lives. We feel that 800 to 1,200 milligrams per day is needed, depending on your age, sex and where you live, for most people to cut the risk of the calcium deficiency diseases that become apparent in adulthood: osteoporosis, hypertension and certain cancers. Currently 85 per cent of women and the majority of men take in less calcium than they need.

The 800 to 1,200 milligrams intake of calcium per day we recommend for most people is in the context of the programme outlined in this book, including intake of eight to twelve glasses of water a day, restriction of foods containing oxalates, and excess salt, which lower calcium absorption, exercise, consultation with a doctor or dietician, and other measures. Excessive intake of salt, especially intake of above 5 grams per day, increases urinary loss of calcium;

high intakes of oxalate may increase risk of kidney stones in some people.

Intake of calcium by men is nearly as poor as by women. Only a small portion take in the levels we recommend.

The amounts of calcium you need are high because the body absorbs so little. Our diet and lifestyle conspire to keep a typical urban adult from absorbing 65 to 85 per cent of the calcium consumed.

Once you have absorbed calcium, your body can send it where it is needed. If you happen to absorb more than you need on a particular day, you will excrete more than usual to balance the high intake. In any event, your body has had a chance to get all the calcium you need. If you do *not* absorb enough calcium, your body will pay the price.

Vitamin D Deficiency

If you take in calcium, but there is too little vitamin D in your body, your body will not be able to absorb most of the calcium. Absorption of calcium is controlled by vitamin D.

When you are very young, your skin can produce vitamin D easily, but as you get older it cannot. Your skin produces half as much vitamin D at the age of sixty as at the age of ten, according to a recent study by Drs J. MacLaughlin and M. Holick of Tufts University School of Medicine in Boston.

Your ability to absorb vitamin D from the food you eat also decreases with age, so it is especially important to take in your diet the suggested amounts of vitamin D recommended in this book for the area in which you live, and your age. A complete profile of your needs can be determined from the information in Chapter 7.

Osteoporosis

If your bones weigh too little for your size, you have low bone mass. If your bone mass is extremely low for your body size, or you have had a fracture due to low bone mass, you are considered to have osteoporosis. The bones have lost so much calcium that they become fragile, brittle and susceptible to fractures. Osteoporosis increases the chances of one or more of your bones breaking one day, perhaps during some minor traumatic event. The bones that usually break are the head of the femur (the bone from your hip to your knee) and the vertebrae, or spinal bones.

Contrary to popular belief, your bones are continuously broken down and rebuilt in your body. Bone dissolvers, or osteoclasts, are constantly tearing bone calcium and protein apart, while cellular building crews, or osteoblasts, work to rebuild it. Some bones are entirely rebuilt or remodelled every five years, some faster.

Nevertheless, although the cells that make up bones are constantly active, bones are *not* at the top of the list in terms of the body's priorities for calcium. Instead, bones are at the bottom of the list. The calcium needs of the body, in terms of priority, are as follows:

Blood	Pancreas
Heart	Kidney
Brain	Liver
Intestine	Skin
Stomach	Bones

Because of this, it is hard to deliver the calcium that *is* absorbed to your bones. The bones are always at the end of the line when the body considers its overall calcium needs.

The problem is made worse because your intestines, if

you are like most adults, will not absorb most of the calcium you take in.

The epidemiology of osteoporosis can best be described by studies of two harmful effects of the disease: fractures of the hip and fractures of the vertebrae. Most 'hip' fractures are actually fractures of the head of the femur. Not all fractures of the head of the femur or vertebrae are due to osteoporosis, but many are.

There are big differences between countries in the incidence of hip fractures (Figure 3.1, page 44). The United States is the world leader in hip fractures for men and women. The differences are not due to differences in age between the populations, because age differences have been taken into account. These results tell us that hip fractures aren't a part of the human condition. If they were, the incidence would be the same everywhere.

In fact, a woman living in Yugoslavia is only one sixth as likely to fracture a hip as a woman in the United States. This is unlikely to be due solely to a genetic difference. Dietary deficiencies or environmental factors, such as a deficiency of light, lead to differences in the amount of vitamin D produced in the body, and, we believe, to increased risk of hip fractures.

A recent study in Yugoslavia illustrated the effect of diet. There are two similar towns in Yugoslavia that differ in an important way: intake of calcium. The towns aren't far apart and they share a rural Yugoslavian culture and way of life. But calcium intake in one city is much higher than in the other. The women and men who live in the high-calcium town have had only *half* the incidence of hip fractures as those in the low-calcium town (see Figure 3.2).

The scientists who studied these villages, Dr V. Matkovic and a group of colleagues, published their results in the *American Journal of Clinical Nutrition*. Studies of

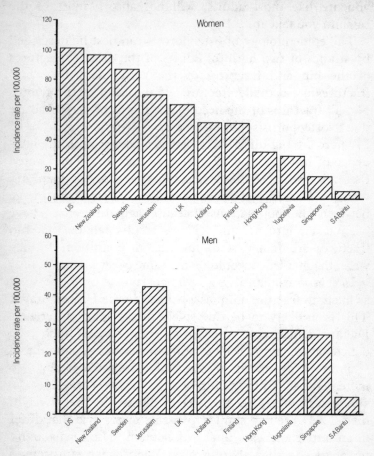

Figure 3.1. Age-adjusted incidence rate of hip fracture per 100,000 people, by location. *Source:* Drawn from data provided in: Cummings S. R., Kelsey J. L., Nevitt M. C., O'Dowd K. J., 'Epidemiology of osteoporosis and osteoporotic fractures', *Epidemiologic Reviews* 1985; 7: 178–208.

bone mass were performed in the two towns and it was found that there was a difference in bone mass that was constant from the earliest age studied to the oldest. This

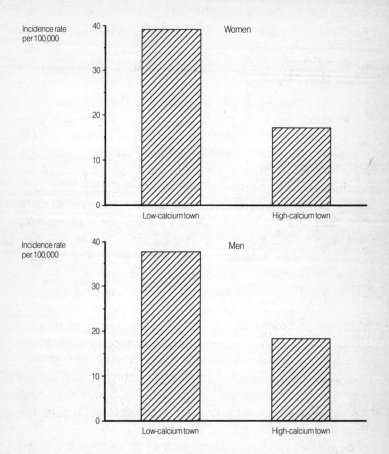

Figure 3.2. Risk of hip fractures in two Yugoslavian towns.
Source: Matkovic V., Kostial K., Simonovic I., et al, 'Bone
status and fracture rates in two regions of Yugoslavia',
American Journal of Clinical Nutrition 1979; 32: 540–49.

suggests that the effect of absorbed calcium is lifelong.
Calcium is needed to form bone. The sooner a calcium-
rich diet is started, the better.

Calcium's Role in the Prevention of Osteoporosis

There are several factors that play a part in the development of osteoporosis. These include being white, female, slender, tall, sedentary, having low oestrogen levels, smoking cigarettes and having a high coffee intake. One reason a woman's bones may become fragile is that she has eaten or absorbed too little calcium throughout her life, gradually depleting the calcium in her bones to make up for the deficiency. American women take in an average of 490 milligrams of calcium a day. This is 10 to 60 milligrams less than the 500 to 550 milligrams of calcium lost each day. When the amount of calcium lost is even slightly more than the amount taken in, bone loss is inevitable. Since 490 milligrams is the *average* daily intake of adult women, we can estimate that about *half* of American women are *losing bone throughout their adult lives*.

The condition is like a dripping tap – the amounts involved are small, but they add up. You may lose only a few milligrams of bone a day, but this loss over several decades will leave you with a substantially reduced skeleton when you reach your sixties or seventies. If you lose 30 per cent to 40 per cent of your bone mass, your spinal column will gradually collapse. You will lose height and may develop 'dowager's hump', a skeletal deformity for which there is no cure.

The role of calcium and vitamin D in the prevention of osteoporosis has not been entirely defined, but it is clear that women should remain in positive calcium balance throughout their lives. They should take in more calcium than they lose each and every day. The question of how much calcium you need and how to overcome a calcium deficiency, is discussed in Chapter 8, and in Part II of the book. According to the British Ministry of Agriculture, Fisheries and Food, the average British person takes in approximately 890 milligrams of calcium each day.

Exercise and Osteoporosis

Calcium and vitamin D will not increase the calcium content of bone without exercise. It is important that you adopt an exercise schedule as well as increase your calcium intake. Exercise makes bones work, strengthens them, even helps to remodel them. The activities of many women and men do not involve sufficient activity in their hip and leg bones. Jobs that minimize use of the lower body, such as sitting at a desk, which many people do for years during their working lives, must be counterbalanced with vigorous activity. A regular routine of weight-bearing exercise is essential.

A walking programme will provide a starting point, but everyone ultimately should work towards a system of aerobic exercises, which provides structural benefits. Low- or non-impact aerobics put a healthy force on the bones of the legs and hips, which are weak points for the development of fractures later in life, without unduly stressing the joints.

Other forms of exercise are less effective. Tennis, for example, does not provide enough mobilization of the long muscles over a sustained period of time to encourage much increased bone mass, and the staccato action of court sports can injure bones and tendons.

Swimming, while it is beneficial to the cardiovascular system and does not put undue pressure on the joints, does not create the necessary weight-bearing loads on the bones of the legs and hips to increase bone mass.

The Plague of Osteoporosis

It is estimated that by the year 2001, 7.5 per cent of the UK population will be aged seventy-five years or more. This means we're going to be facing even more osteoporosis in the future.

Currently, in America nearly one third of the women

residents of nursing homes are there because of fractures, and 85 per cent of these are fractures of the hip. The fractures often follow some minor trauma that would normally not cause a broken hip. But because these women aged sixty and older have fragile bones, a minor fall, or even stepping off a kerb awkwardly, can result in a broken hip. These women may not be aware that they have the crippling disease until the first fracture.

The consequences are serious. This is because a broken hip often requires a period of immobilization, and this can be deadly. Extensive time in bed can sometimes result in pneumonia or the development of blood clots, either of which can be fatal; a third of women will die within a year of an osteoporotic hip fracture.

Oestrogen

Oestrogen also plays a role in the prevention of osteoporosis. Like vitamin D, it enhances the absorption rate of calcium in the intestine, and stops the bones from getting smaller. The reason why it has such an effect is not completely understood. Because oestrogen is beneficial, it is often prescribed to women suffering from osteoporosis, although, like most doctors, we would like to minimize the use of medication. Women with osteoporosis, especially if they are beyond the menopause, frequently need oestrogen to prevent further bone loss and possible fractures. Before the menopause, women's natural oestrogen levels provide protection. Oestrogen stimulates the absorption of calcium by the intestine and also seems to have its own effect in helping bones to maintain their mass and strength.

The use of oestrogen has certain risks. Cancer of the endometrium (part of the uterus) appears to be increased by use of oestrogen, and the incidence of blood clots may be slightly higher in some women who receive the hormone. This is counterbalanced by a lower rate of heart disease in women taking supplementary oestrogens. We understand the fear many women have of endometrial cancer. But women past the menopause are at least ten times more likely to die from heart disease than from endometrial cancer. The benefits of oestrogen in minimizing the harm of osteoporosis may outweigh its risks. Of course, women who have had hysterectomies need not worry about uterine cancer.

The question of oestrogen use and breast cancer is highly controversial. Some scientists have found no risk of breast cancer associated with its use, but a few have found a slight increase in women who have used oestrogens for more than five years. For this reason we recommend that oestrogens be used in as small a dose as possible under consultation by your doctor, for no more than five years, and only if it is determined that there has been sufficient bone loss to justify using it.

The only way to find out if you have suffered bone loss to a degree that necessitates oestrogen treatment is by new procedures that examine selected bones using a far lower dose of X-rays than previous procedures. These methods provide a rapid identification of osteoporosis, and are now becoming widely available. Any woman should consider having an evaluation of her bone status performed at the time of her menopause, whether or not she has symptoms. Osteoporosis frequently does not produce obvious symptoms to the patient until a fall or other trauma results in a fracture, yet early treatment can be quite successful.

Summary

Most people throughout the western world consume far less calcium than they need. The result is that we accelerate the epidemic of calcium-deficiency-related diseases that

strike in adulthood – osteoporosis, hypertension and cancers of the intestine and breast. The risk of some very
serious and disabling diseases can be reduced by increasing
your level of *absorbed* calcium. Part II of this book, The
Calcium Diet Programme, will show you how.

CHAPTER FOUR

CALCIUM AND BLOOD PRESSURE

In the UK, 20 per cent of middle-aged men and 12 per cent of middle-aged women are estimated to suffer from high blood pressure. Furthermore, it has been shown that 20 per cent of men and women aged fifty-five to sixty-four years are receiving drug treatment for this condition. There is a chance that you will develop it in the future, and you might have it now. In recent years, research studies have shown a connection between blood pressure and calcium. It is yet another way in which calcium plays a crucial role in your body's health.

Blood pressure is measured by the number of millimetres a column of mercury rises in a blood-pressure monitor. The first number, the systolic blood pressure, refers to the blood pressure in the arteries while the heart is contracting and pumping blood into them. The second number, the diastolic blood pressure, is blood pressure between heartbeats, while the heart is resting. In other words, the systolic reading measures your maximum blood pressure and the diastolic measures your minimum blood pressure at the time the pressure is tested. A normal blood-pressure reading is considered to be 120/80.

High blood pressure, though it may cause no noticeable symptoms, is very serious. It can cause kidney disease, stroke and heart disease. Every ten points above 140/90 doubles your risk of death. This is why it is often called the silent killer.

Calcium and Blood Pressure

Several studies have shown that people who take in high amounts of calcium – 1,200 milligrams per day – have a lower blood pressure and fewer health problems than people who consume smaller amounts of calcium. In America the typical adult woman consumes 491 milligrams of calcium per day and the typical adult man consumes 724 milligrams per day. People in Britain consume somewhat more.

A US government survey found that adults taking in 500 milligrams or less of calcium per day had twice the risk of hypertension as those consuming 1,500 milligrams per day or more.

The connection between calcium and blood pressure was backed by a Rancho Bernardo, California, study, a fifteen-year study of adult residents of a suburban community near San Diego, initiated by Elizabeth Barrett-Connor and her colleagues at the University of California, San Diego. It showed that men who drank three or more glasses of milk a day (a food rich in calcium) had average blood pressures of 134/78, while those who consumed two glasses or less per day had average pressures of 137/81. This is a difference of three points in the systolic and diastolic blood pressure. A clinical trial of blood-pressure medication by the British Medical Research Council reported in the *British Medical Journal* in 1985 that a ten-point drop in blood pressure cut the risk of stroke virtually by half.

A test by David A. McCarron and colleagues of the Oregon Health Sciences University (1985) concluded that 1,000 milligrams of calcium taken every day for eight weeks lowered blood pressure in men and women with mild hypertension by about *five* points.

Several theories exist to explain how calcium lowers

blood pressure, though none of them has yet been proven. People with normal blood pressures don't appear to lower their blood pressure by taking in higher levels of calcium. This suggests that people with hypertension suffer from a deficiency of calcium – which may mean they have trouble absorbing the calcium they take in. It may also mean that such people have abnormalities in the way their cells absorb calcium.

Vitamin D, which aids in the body's ability to absorb and use calcium, may play a role in regulation of blood pressure. A study by Mary Fran Sowers and colleagues at the University of Iowa (1985) found that women under thirty-five who took 400 IU per day of vitamin D had systolic blood pressure six points lower than those who took in smaller amounts – an average of 111/69 compared to 117/69. They found that younger women who consumed the recommended amount of vitamin D also took in higher levels of calcium, usually from milk. Sowers attributed one point of the blood-pressure drop to intake of calcium and the rest to vitamin D. Her group also analysed the effects of body weight and alcohol intake, but found that it was vitamin D which had the greatest effect.

Preventing and Controlling Hypertension

Large numbers of people with high blood pressure have readings only moderately above normal, between 120/80 and 150/95. If you are in this category, you may be able to reduce your blood pressure and maintain it by changing your lifestyle, instead of relying on medication. This has been confirmed by the long-term Framingham (Massachusetts) Heart Study and other studies in Illinois and Minnesota. These studies show that with goal-setting and guidance, many people who formerly took medication can maintain normal blood pressure by lifestyle changes alone. Also, people who currently need medication can often greatly reduce their dose levels if they make changes in their diet and lifestyle.

There are many ways to help lower blood pressure without drugs. First, *lose weight*. If you're 20 per cent overweight, you are twice as likely to develop hypertension as someone with normal weight. Every pound you shed results in a drop of one point in blood pressure. Dieting and maintaining the lower weight is one of the most effective ways of overcoming and controlling hypertension.

Second, *reduce your use of salt*. No one with high blood pressure should eat more than 2,500 milligrams of salt a day. According to the British Heart Foundation, most people require only 600 milligrams of salt daily.

Third, *stop smoking*. Smoking increases risk of arteriosclerosis (hardening of the arteries) and risk of stroke.

Fourth, *raise your potassium level*. Take in 3,000 milligrams a day by including more potassium-rich foods in your diet. Appendix F lists some of the best sources of potassium. It includes a lot of foods that you probably eat anyway.

Fifth, *increase your calcium intake to the levels we recommend* (see chart on page 85). You may be able to drop your blood pressure by 8 to 10 points if you both raise your potassium intake to 3,000 milligrams and your calcium intake as recommended.

Sixth, *increase your intake of vitamin D to the level we recommend* (see chart on page 86). This amount of vitamin D may cut your blood-pressure reading by several more points, particularly if you are a woman. Calcium must be absorbed in order to reduce your blood pressure, and vitamin D helps your body to absorb the calcium you take in and make it usable. You'll find a complete programme and further guidelines to help you increase your calcium intake and absorption in the chapters to follow in *The Calcium Diet*.

Maintaining Your Blood Pressure

You may want to monitor your blood pressure to make sure it is actually being reduced by changes in your diet and lifestyle. Going to the doctor every few months to have it checked is a good idea. But blood-pressure readings at the doctor's office can be misleading, as patients are often anxious in the setting of the consulting room; acute anxiety temporarily raises blood pressure in some people. Although some doctors try to take the anxiety factor into account, it is difficult to judge because it varies greatly from patient to patient. If your blood pressure reading is high as a result, your doctor may prescribe a course of action that is inappropriate.

The best idea for someone with high blood pressure is to buy a blood-pressure measuring machine (known by the daunting name sphygmomanometer). They can be purchased at many pharmacies. Any doctor or nurse can teach you how to use one. You might set up an informal appointment with your practice nurse during a quiet time at the office and take the twenty minutes or so that you'll need to learn how to use it. Then take readings in the relaxed atmosphere of your home every two weeks or so. Always take the reading at the same time of day, as blood pressure may go up or down somewhat during the day. Keep a record and you'll know how well your diet routine is working. Be sure to bring your record along whenever you see your doctor; it will be valuable information for him or her about the success of your control programme.

If lifestyle changes alone do not work, your doctor may

prescribe medication. One common drug used is a diuretic that will cut down excessive amounts of fluid and sodium in your tissues, and increase the amount of calcium your body retains in the fluid bathing your cells. Even if you must take drugs, you can lower the dosage by increasing your calcium and potassium intake.

CHAPTER FIVE

CALCIUM ROBBERS

As we've mentioned previously, there is an enormous difference between the calcium you take in daily and the amount of usable calcium that your body can absorb. Until now, all calcium tables and values printed on food packages and other literature on calcium have been based on crude laboratory methods. They show you how much calcium is *present*, but do not show you how much is *usable*.

Peanut butter is a perfect example of this. This popular food is listed in existing nutritional tables as having about 60 milligrams of calcium per serving. You'd think from this that it would therefore be a useful source of calcium. But none of the calcium in peanut butter can be absorbed and used by your body. Worse, we believe peanut butter actually *steals* 164 milligrams of calcium per serving from foods eaten with it or within a few hours of eating it.

Many foods 'steal' calcium. We call such foods calcium robbers. How do they do it? The molecules of calcium robbers bond extremely easily to calcium. They will readily abandon another element for calcium should they come into contact with calcium. Phytate, a molecule in certain nuts, seeds and vegetables is a prime example. Phytate is usually bound to sodium or other elements. However, when it comes into contact with a calcium molecule, it will desert the other element it is attached to and bond with the calcium. The problem is that when calcium is bound to phytate, the body is usually unable to unbind the two molecules, and the calcium passes through the small intestine in an unusable form until it is excreted from the body. The calcium might just as well have not been eaten.

Similar to phytate is oxalate, another molecule that binds with calcium and makes it unusable. Many foods contain phytates and oxalates, and it is these foods that we term calcium robbers. Eating such foods with calcium-rich foods negates the potential benefits of a calcium-rich diet.

The worst calcium robbers are as follows:

Robber	Mg of calcium lost per 3.5 ounce serving
Wheat bran	−350
Swiss chard	−220
Brazil nuts	−198
Spinach	−166
Peanut butter	−163
Peanuts	−163
Shredded wheat	−157
Barley	−90
Tea (cup, steeped 6 minutes)	−60
Walnuts	−59
Coconut	−37
Bulgur wheat (a rough Middle Eastern cooked wheat)	−35
Beetroot	−34
Pecans	−19
Oats	−17

The Special Case of Wheat Bran

You may be surprised to see wheat bran at the top of the calcium-robber list. The tendency of wheat bran to bind calcium has long been known. Scientists since the 1930s have fed wheat-bran-rich foods to animals to induce rickets.

Recent studies for the US Department of Agriculture by Dr June Kelsay involved feeding whole wheat bran cakes to volunteers who were eating diets containing about 1,100 milligrams of calcium per day. One day's intake consisted of a total of one ounce of wheat bran, which was baked into cakes served two to a meal. During the experiment, the researchers found that the volunteers absorbed only 15 per cent of the calcium in their diets, which was much less than half of what was expected. An astounding 85 per cent of the calcium was lost. As the experiment went on, the volunteers adapted to the dose of bran they received. But in the meantime, calcium absorption suffered.

Many of us eat foods rich in wheat bran sporadically. When we do, the bran acts as a potent calcium binder and robs our bodies of at least half of the calcium we would normally absorb from other foods. A week-long binge on wheat-bran-rich food once a month could cause you to miss out on as much as 500 milligrams of the calcium you ate each day.

Because phytate was the first suspect in the test volunteers' calcium loss, scientists removed the phytate from the bran muffins used in the experiment. When the phytate was taken out of the bran, there was *still* a 20 per cent decrease in calcium absorption. This is how we know that bran has a calcium-robbing effect independent of its phytate. We know that 80 per cent of this calcium theft is due to phytate; the rest is due to other chemical thieves in wheat bran, some of which have not yet been identified.

The information above may be perplexing because many doctors and nutritionists have recommended wheat bran as a way to prevent colon cancer. But these recommendations were based mostly on comparisons of the risk of colon cancer in Africa with other parts of the world, including some studies which focused on fibre from fruits and vegetables, but not on wheat bran specifically. Although Africans do eat fibre-rich diets, we believe that the secret of Africa's low rates of colon cancer may be the sunlight it receives and the resulting high levels of vitamin D – Africa is the sunniest place on the face of the earth. And we believe that wheat bran does not especially lower the rate of colon cancer.

Our review of epidemiological results of a major, well-designed and scrupulously conducted study reported in the *Journal of the National Cancer Institute* by Dr Baruch Modan and his co-workers in Israel (1975) revealed that certain foods increased the risk of colon cancer. The foods seemed to fit no known pattern and the reason for their effects was not understood at the time.

The foods that were shown to increase risk of intestinal cancer in the Israeli study were:

Spinach
Walnuts
Oats
Bulgur wheat

These are foods we now know to be some of the strongest binders of calcium in nature – and all are calcium robbers. It's not surprising that people who ate large amounts of them developed colon cancer. Some of the foods that have been most highly recommended in the past may actually be some of the worst offenders.

Protein, Sugar and Calcium

High intake of protein will also cause you to lose calcium. If you eat more than 120 grams of protein per day you begin to enter a dietary range where the protein will cause calcium loss. We estimate that you will lose 50 to 70 milligrams of calcium per day for each 30 grams of protein you eat above 120 grams. This can make a big difference if you're an avid steak or meat eater. If so, you'll need to eat additional amounts of foods in your diet that are rich in calcium to make up the difference.

Heavy intake of sugar will also cause you to lose calcium through excess excretion. The exact relationship between sugar and calcium is still being evaluated, but if you eat more than 60 grams per day of sugar, honey or other sugars in any form, you'll need to add calcium above the usual requirements to your diet. Until more research is completed, we recommend that you add 100 milligrams of calcium to your diet for each 30 grams of sugar you consume over 60 grams per day. Don't forget to count the sugar in soft drinks, flavoured yogurts, sweets, ice cream and syrups in canned fruit. We recommend that you eventually try to cut your intake of sugar to much less than two ounces per day.

Coffee and Tea

Coffee, tea and alcohol also have an important effect on calcium absorption. One reason is that we drink so much of them. Water was once our favourite drink, but no longer. The typical British person uses 50 grams of tea (dry weight) and 20 grams of coffee (dry weight) each week just in their homes. Although Britain is considered to be a nation of tea drinkers, coffee is now brewed in many British homes. Some people drink ten to twenty cups per day. Step into any cafe, or even a tea shop, and the waitress will ask with a smile, 'Coffee?' Your answer should usually be, 'No, thanks.'

Each cup of coffee causes you to lose about 10 milligrams of calcium. This may not seem like a lot, but the loss may mean trouble if your calcium intake is already low. Most people who take in less than 500 to 600 milligrams of calcium per day are *losing* calcium from their bodies. This amount just isn't sufficient to maintain a positive calcium balance according to sophisticated studies using a tracing method based on a calcium isotope, such as that reported by Dr H. Spencer and her colleagues in the *American Journal of Medicine* (1985).

A large proportion of Britons don't take in as much as 600 milligrams of calcium per day. If your calcium intake is low, coffee could cause problems over time. Five cups of coffee per day could subtract 50 milligrams of calcium, calcium that will come from your bones.

If you want to keep drinking coffee, it is important that you increase your calcium intake by 10 to 20 milligrams per day for each cup of coffee that you drink.

One solution is to add skimmed milk to the coffee when you drink it. Don't use cream, however, or your fat intake will increase. Equally bad, or possibly even worse, is to add non-dairy creamer to your coffee. This will give you a large dose of coconut oil or other heavily hydrogenated oils that can cause an increase in blood cholesterol. The best answer of all is to stop drinking coffee, or cut down to a maximum of two cups per day.

There seems to be some increase of risk of certain cancers for people who drink coffee in large quantities. The effect is not dramatic, but it seems significant. We have also worked on studies of the effect of coffee on cholesterol in your blood. Perhaps surprisingly, coffee seems to increase plasma cholesterol, particularly in women. Our research group recently studied a large group of women in southern California and found that women who drank four cups of coffee per day had plasma cholesterol levels about 15 per cent higher than women who drank less than one cup per day.

There is no conclusive evidence that the harmful effects of coffee on risk of cancer or increased plasma cholesterol are due solely to caffeine, since some effects appear to be present even for decaffeinated coffee. So far it is not known which of the hundreds of chemicals found in coffee may be responsible for its health risks. But it seems clear that the less coffee you drink, the healthier you'll be.

Many people respond to the potential health hazards of coffee with the comment, 'If I can't drink coffee, I'll have tea.' Some British people drink ten or more cups of tea each day. The effect of tea on calcium in your diet depends on how the tea is prepared. If you brew the tea for a long time – six minutes – you will lose 60 milligrams of calcium for every cup you drink. Regular intake of even one cup per day could cause you to lose calcium from bone if your dietary intake of calcium is low. One solution is to brew the tea for less time. Cutting the duration of brewing to two minutes will reduce calcium loss to 20 milligrams per cup. This is still a lot and you should seriously consider cutting your intake of tea if you drink more than a cup or two per day. Herbal tea may be an answer for you, though we suggest you avoid some of the very exotic herbal teas, which may contain other toxic compounds.

What about diet or sugar-free soft drinks? Sugar-free soft drinks have become one of the most popular beverages in Britain. There are no data that we have found showing a large amount of calcium loss from artificially sweetened drinks.

Alcohol

The verdict on alcohol and its effect on calcium is not much better than that for tea or coffee. The Scotch you may look forward to each night while relaxing in your slippers with your dog contains no calcium. People who drink a lot of alcohol tend to absorb vitamin D and calcium from their diet poorly. One result for those who drink a lot of alcohol is bone loss, even in young people. It is amazing how you can accelerate a process that leads to loss of bone by drinking alcohol, even when you are young.

Alcohol consumption has also been linked to risk of colon cancer, a relationship we observed in our study of the 1,954 Western Electric workers. Numerous other scientists have reported a similar effect. There are changes in the microscopic structure of the intestine of people who drink a lot of alcohol that make it hard for vitamin D to pass through the fine structures of the cells. The ultimate result is that the calcium is not absorbed, which causes an increase in the rate of cell division of the intestinal wall.

Moderate intake of wine may not harm calcium absorption. Recent studies show that men who drink a moderate amount of wine have no trouble absorbing calcium, although the results are not definitive. In fact, including a small amount of alcohol in your life may have positive health benefits. A number of studies have shown that people who drink a small amount of alcohol – no more than one and a half glasses of wine a day, or its equivalent in beer or spirits – have 40 per cent fewer deaths from heart disease and stroke than people who don't drink at all. The key is moderation. Remember that if you do consume modest amounts of alcohol, you should increase your calcium intake accordingly.

CHAPTER SIX

CALCIUM TRANSPORTERS

Calcium and Pectin

Not all foods that bind calcium act as robbers. Some substances found in food act more as calcium transporters – gently carrying calcium molecules to the large intestine. Foremost of the transporters is pectin, a substance found in many fruits and vegetables, particularly in apples.

Pectin refers to both pectin and its relatives, the polysaccharides, in fruits and vegetables that aren't derived from cellulose or its relatives or starch.

The Latin root word polysaccharide means 'many sugars'. These sugars are bound together so they can't be absorbed by your body. Your body is able to absorb free sugars such as fructose (fruit sugar), sucrose (table sugar), maltose (honey sugar), lactose (milk sugar), and glucose (a sugar found in carrots and other vegetables). However, the body would need a special enzyme to break the polysaccharides into these smaller free sugars, and our bodies don't have the enzyme to do it. But it doesn't leave your body, either. It does something even more important.

Pectin is a faithful carrier of calcium to your large intestine. It does this with a molecular structure that looks and acts like an egg crate.

If you looked at pectin in its pure state (you can buy it at a grocery shop), you'd find that it is a light-coloured powder. It has a fascinating molecular structure that consists of a long chain of up to a thousand units of a simple plant acid. It looks like one of the long dragons that zig-zag through a Chinese New Year parade.

If you add calcium to pectin, a gel forms. One ounce of pectin gel contains *750 milligrams* of calcium in its molecular egg crate. Because we don't have an enzyme in our bodies that will break down pectin in our stomach or small intestine, it passes through those organs intact to the large intestine.

How does pectin in an apple work? Once the stomach has broken down the apple (which it does in about twenty minutes) the dissolved apple next moves into the small intestine, which absorbs the nutrients in the apple along its twenty-five-foot length. Most of the apple gets absorbed in a few minutes. After travelling through the small intestine, all that's left of the apple are three compounds: cellulose, lignin and pectin. Cellulose and lignin are the compounds that make up the woody parts of the plant cell wall. They're unusable by the body and pass through untouched until they are eliminated. Pectin, however, is another matter.

Pectin next enters the large intestine, where friendly bacteria take it apart and use it as a source of fuel for themselves. They are able to do this because they have an enzyme we don't. Although bacteria eat pectin, it has no caloric value to us.

What, then, is the advantage of pectin? Pectin molecules embrace calcium in their egg-carton construction, making fruits and vegetables pleasantly firm and springy. The more calcium dissolved in pectin, the springier the fruit or vegetable. Scientists believe pectin's egg-crate shape is the reason for its ability to safely deliver calcium to the large intestine.

Some nutritionists believe that compounds in grain, fruits and vegetables protect the intestine by making its contents move through quickly. The theory is that shorter exposure of the foods to the intestine allows less time for any carcinogens foods might contain to affect the cells of the intestine.

Dr Gary Glober, a gastroenterologist, performed a study in the late 1970s of transit time, or the amount of time it takes for a meal to pass through the intestine, to find out if the theory is true. Foods can take anywhere from four to thirty-six hours to pass through the intestine of a person on a typical western diet.

Glober wanted to find out whether populations who had low cancer rates of the large intestine had fast transit times. To test the idea, he compared the transit times of foods passing through the intestines of Japanese people, who have a low intestinal cancer rate, with Caucasians, who have a relatively high intestinal cancer rate. Much to scientists' surprise, Glober found there was no significant difference in transit time between the low-risk cancer population and the high-risk cancer population. Research reported by Dr D. J. A. Jenkins in the *British Medical Journal* in 1978 showed that some types of fibre actually delayed transit time.

Another theory was that fibre increased the bulk of material in the intestine and somehow diluted the carcinogens that might be present in food. It is a plausible idea, but we now know that there are many groups of people who do not eat large amounts of grain, fruits and vegetables and have very low rates of intestinal cancer. Japanese people, for example, are a case in point. They eat a diet full of fish, polished rice and other low-bulk foods, yet they have extremely low incidence of intestinal cancer.

After reviewing classic studies conducted by our colleagues Baruch Modan in Israel (1975); Roland Phillips, Jan Kuzma and David Snowden in California (1985); and Saxon Graham at Roswell Park Memorial Institute in

Buffalo, New York (1978), we conclude that fruits and vegetables protect against intestinal cancers.

We now believe that it is pectin, the compound found in apples and other fruits and vegetables, which contributes heavily to prevention of intestinal cancer. It does so by delivering a large amount of calcium directly to the large intestine. In the acidic medium of the large intestine in many people the calcium is absorbed for use by other parts of the body, and also directly benefits the cells of the intestine's walls as it passes through them.

There may be another benefit of pectin. When it is digested by friendly acidic bacteria that live in the large intestine, it releases calcium. The calcium, in turn, appears to be slowly absorbed by the intestine while some of it reacts with fatty acids, bile salts and other carcinogens in the intestine to form inert compounds called soaps. The soaps do not react with the lining of your large intestine, so there's no damage. Calcium binds up the attackers, rendering them unable to harm the intestinal cells. With a plentiful supply of calcium in the large intestine, the rate of cell divison along the lining of the large intestine drops.

Pectins, in other words, act to transport calcium safely and effectively to the large intestine, where it can be slowly absorbed and used in the body, and where it can interact with potentially dangerous carcinogens to neutralize them.

We strongly suggest that you include in your diet as many foods that are rich in pectin as possible. Apples, oranges, lemons, limes, grapefruits, kiwi fruit and a wide range of fruits, as well as most vegetables, contain substantial amounts of pectin. The following is a list of some of the foods which have high amounts of pectin in them.

FOOD HIGH IN PECTIN*

Food	Milligrams per serving
Broccoli	15
Green or white cabbage	15
Citrus fruits with pulp	14
Runner or French beans	13
Kale	13
Brussels sprouts	13
Cucumber	13
Carrots	13
Red cabbage	11
Tomatoes	11
Cauliflower	11
Strawberries	10
Onions	8
Raspberries	8
Broad beans	8
Currants	7
Prunes	7
Apples with peel	6
Pears with peel	5
Potatoes, new	5

*Pectin and related compounds.

Source: Adapted from Hans Englyst, 'Determination of Carbohydrate and Its Composition in Plant Materials', in W. P. T. James and Olof Theander (eds): *The Analysis of Dietary Fiber in Food*. New York, Marcel Dekker, Inc., 1981.

CHAPTER SEVEN

YOUR CALCIUM PROFILE

How much calcium and vitamin D do you need in your diet to minimize the dangers of osteoporosis, high blood pressure and cancer? As you have seen in the preceding chapters, your individual calcium and vitamin D needs vary according to your age, whether you are a man or a woman, according to what part of the country you live in, and according to your lifestyle. The purpose of this chapter is to help design the optimal programme for *you*.

Choose a quiet time and a relaxed atmosphere to fill in the profiles. You'll probably need your pocket calculator, too.

There are three profiles:

The Environmental Vitamin D Profile
The Dietary Vitamin D Profile
The Calcium Profile

The Environmental Vitamin D Profile

This profile asks a few questions about your habits and provides you with an Environmental Vitamin D score which you can use to determine how much dietary vitamin D you'll need. Look at the map on page 74 to discover your environmental vitamin D factor; this is given by region so your number corresponds to the number of the region nearest your home.

If, like most people, you spend a lot of time indoors, you'll need more dietary vitamin D and calcium. If you live in an area of the country with a high level of air pollution, you'll need more, too. Filling out the profile helps to tailor the right diet for *you*. And it should only take about fifteen to twenty minutes to finish.

The Environmental Vitamin D Profile

Instructions: Circle the number of points as directed for each season. You will add the points at the end of the profile to calculate your environmental vitamin D score.

1. Circle the *number of points* under the best estimate of how many *minutes* you spend *outdoors* * on a typical *weekday* between 9 a.m. and 3 p.m.

Minutes spent outdoors on a typical weekday

Season	Less than 8	8 to 15	More than 15
Summer	3 points	16 points	18 points
Autumn/Spring	2 points	8 points	10 points
Winter	1 point	5 points	7 points

*Outdoors in the sun or shade even on a cloudy day. Time spent in a car is not considered outdoors unless the car is a convertible with the top down.

2. Circle the *number of points* below the description which is closest to what you wear when you are outdoors between 9 a.m. and 3 p.m. on a typical *weekday*. If you spend less than 8 minutes on a typical weekday in a season, circle zero points for that season.

What you wear when outdoors during the week

Season	Long sleeves, long trousers or skirt	Short sleeves, long trousers or skirt	Short sleeves, or no shirt, shorts
Summer	0 points	4 points	8 points
Autumn/ Spring	0 points	2 points	4 points
Winter	0 points	1 point	2 points

3. Circle the *number of points* below the best estimate of how many *minutes* you spend *outdoors*★ on a typical *weekend* day between 9 a.m. and 3 p.m.

Minutes spent outdoors on a typical weekend day

Season	Less than 8	8 to 15	More than 15
Summer	1 point	6 points	7 points
Autumn/Spring	1 point	3 points	4 points
Winter	0 points	2 points	3 points

★Outdoors in the sun or shade even on a cloudy day. Time spent in a car is not considered outdoors unless the car is a convertible with the top down.

4. Circle the number of points below the description that is closest to what you wear when you are outdoors between 9 a.m. and 3 p.m. on a typical *weekend* day. If you spend less than 8 minutes on a typical weekend day in a season, circle zero points for that season.

What you wear when outdoors on weekends

Season	Long sleeves, long trousers or skirt	Short sleeves, long trousers or skirt	Short sleeves, or no shirt, shorts
Summer	0 points	2 points	3 points
Autumn/ Spring	0 points	1 point	2 points
Winter	0 points	0 points	1 point

Now add the numbers you have circled. Here is a worksheet.

Question	Points
1. Summer	_____
Autumn/Spring	_____
Winter	_____

2. Summer   _____
   Autumn/Spring   _____
   Winter   _____

3. Summer   _____
   Autumn/Spring   _____
   Winter   _____

4. Summer   _____
   Autumn/Spring   _____
   Winter   _____

Total (add column)   _____ (A)

Use the map on page 74 and find the points for the area where you live, and write the number here _____(B)

Now you are ready for the last step.

MULTIPLY (A) times (B) and write your answer here _____ (C)

This is your *Environmental Vitamin D Score*, and you will use it later to calculate your Total Vitamin D Score.

The Dietary Vitamin D Profile

A portion of the vitamin D your body uses comes from diet, so a profile for it is needed. The next profile asks you how many servings of vitamin D-containing foods you eat or drink in a typical week. Fill in the number of servings of each food that you have in a typical week. If you never have a typical week, just fill in your best estimate.

One serving of any food is 3.5 ounces. If you ate 7 ounces, you ate two servings; 11 ounces equals three servings. Less than 2 ounces equals roughly half a serving.

If you eat one serving every *two* weeks, write in $\frac{1}{2}$

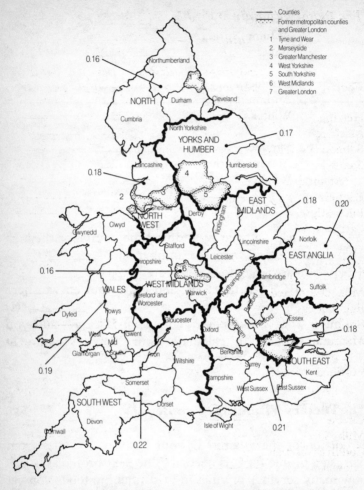

Figure 7.1. Ultraviolet 'Zone Scores' for England and Wales by Drs Cedric and Frank Garland for the British edition of *The Calcium Diet* with Ellen Thro and the assistance of Eva Garliano.

serving (or 0.5 if using a calculator). If you eat a food once a month, write in ¼ serving (or 0.25). Round your answer to the nearest whole number.

The Dietary Vitamin D Profile

Food	Number of servings per week	Multiply by	Points per serving	Total points
Herring	_____	×	135 =	_____
Mackerel	_____	×	105 =	_____
Salmon (Pacific)	_____	×	75 =	_____
Salmon (Atlantic)	_____	×	1 =	_____
Kippers	_____	×	70 =	_____
Pilchards	_____	×	48 =	_____
Sardines, anchovies	_____	×	45 =	_____
Margarine	_____	×	45 =	_____
Tuna	_____	×	35 =	_____
Milk, evaporated	_____	×	17 =	_____
Egg (per egg)	_____	×	15 =	_____
Shrimp	_____	×	15 =	_____
Margarine (2 pats)	_____	×	13 =	_____
Fortified spreads (2 pats)	_____	×	13 =	_____
Liver (any type)	_____	×	6 =	_____
Cheese	_____	×	2 =	_____
Milk (8 oz)	_____	×	1 =	_____
Cod liver oil (per tablespoon)	_____	×	175 =	_____

Total (add column)   _____(D)

This is your *Dietary Vitamin D Score*.

Write your *Dietary Vitamin D Score* here . . . . . .   _____(D)

Write your *Environmental Vitamin D Score* here   _____(C)

ADD (D) and (C) and write total here . . . .   _____(E)
This is your *Total Vitamin D Score*.

Interpreting your *Total Vitamin D Score*.

If your score is:	Your total vitamin D level is:	Comments:
250 or more	Desirable	You are getting enough vitamin D for a typical adult.
200 to 249	Borderline	You may need more vitamin D to be protected from the calcium-deficiency diseases discussed in the book. The diets in this book will bring your intake up to the desirable level.
150 to 199	Deficient	You are not getting enough vitamin D to minimize your risk of a calcium-deficiency disease. Begin diets in the book today to bring your intake up to the desirable level.
149 or less	Seriously deficient	You are getting very little vitamin D, increasing your risk of osteoporosis and breast and intestinal cancer.

We do not recommend that you increase your exposure to the sun to raise your vitamin D level.

The Quick-take Calcium Profile

Vitamin D can be obtained from time spent outdoors in the light, or from diet, but this isn't true for calcium. Most calcium is concentrated in a surprisingly small number of foods and beverages. Partly because of this, almost all of us consume much less calcium than we need.

By completing the following quick-take calcium profile,

you will know exactly where you stand on calcium intake. The profile will take another ten minutes to complete, but it will be well worth your time.

Foods High in Calcium (These are listed in alphabetical order.) Write in the number of servings of each food you eat or drink in a typical week. If you eat one serving every two weeks, write $\frac{1}{2}$ (or 0.5 if using a calculator); if you eat the food once a month, write $\frac{1}{4}$ (or 0.25); if less often, write zero.

High-calcium Foods
(Foods with 250 mg of calcium or more per serving)

Food	Number of servings per week
Brick cheese (2 oz)	_____
Cheddar cheese (2 oz)	_____
Colby cheese (2 oz)	_____
Feta cheese (2 oz)	_____
Goat cheese (3 oz)	_____
Gouda cheese (2 oz)	_____
Gruyère cheese (1 oz)	_____
Mozzarella cheese (2 oz)	_____
Muenster cheese (2 oz)	_____
Parmesan cheese (1 oz)	_____
Processed cheese (2 oz)	_____
Romano cheese (1 oz)	_____
Swiss cheese (1 oz)	_____
Buttermilk (8-oz glass)	_____
Semi-skimmed milk (8 oz)	_____
Skimmed milk (8 oz)	_____
Whole milk (8 oz)	_____
Sardines (3 oz)	_____
Yogurt, plain (8 oz)	_____
	_____
Total (add column)	_____ (F)

MULTIPLY the total number of servings (F) of high calcium foods by 4 and write your answer here _____(G)

This is your number of points from *high-calcium foods*; you will use this number later to calculate your total calcium intake.

Foods Moderately High in Calcium
(Foods with less than 120 mg of calcium per serving)
(One serving is 3.5 oz, except as shown.)

Food	Number of servings per week
Anchovies	_____
Artichokes	_____
Asparagus	_____
Bread and rolls	_____
Broccoli	_____
Cabbage (6 oz)	_____
Carrots (6 oz)	_____
Cauliflower	_____
Celery	_____
Blue or Roquefort cheese (1 oz)	_____
Brie cheese	_____
Camembert cheese	_____
Chicory	_____
Cottage cheese	_____
Edam cheese (1 oz)	_____
Ricotta cheese (2 oz)	_____
Chives (1 oz)	_____
Clams, raw	_____
Cream puff with custard	_____
Cream, single	_____
Cream, light whipping	_____
Cucumber	_____
Custard	_____
Eclair	_____
Egg (one)	_____
Endive	_____

Figs, dried   _____
Herring   _____
Ice cream   _____
Kale   _____
Lettuce   _____
Lobster   _____
Macaroni and cheese   _____
Muffins   _____
Mussels   _____
Oranges   _____
Oysters   _____
Pancakes   _____
Peas (6 oz)   _____
Peapods   _____
Pears (6 oz)   _____
Peaches (6 oz)   _____
Pineapple (6 oz)   _____
Pizza (1 slice)   _____
Salmon (6 oz)   _____
Shrimp (2 oz)   _____
Tofu   _____
Tomato   _____
Tuna   _____
Yogurt, with fruit (6 oz)   _____

    Total (add column)   _____ (H)

This total is your number of points from *moderately high-calcium foods*.

Write *moderately high-calcium food* points here   _____ (H)

Write *high-calcium food* points here (from page 78)   _____ (G)

ADD (H) and (G) and write total here   _____ (I)

These are your total points from *calcium foods*.

Some foods bind calcium and make it unabsorbable. These are calcium robbers. We have divided calcium robbers into two groups based on how much calcium they steal: Calcium Villains and Calcium Henchmen.

Calcium Villains
(Foods stealing 60 to 350 mg of calcium per serving)
(One serving is 3.5 oz)

Food	Number of servings per week
Barley	_____
Bran	_____
Brazil nuts	_____
Peanut butter	_____
Peanuts	_____
Swede	_____
Shredded wheat	_____
Spinach	_____
Swiss chard	_____
Tea (8 fluid oz brewed 6 minutes or more)	_____
Total (add column)	_____(J)

MULTIPLY the total number of servings (J) of Calcium Villains by 2 and write your answer here   _____ (K)

This is your number of points from *Calcium Villains*.

Calcium Henchmen
(Foods stealing 10 to 59 mg of calcium per serving)
(One serving is 3.5 oz)

Food	Number of servings per week
Almonds	_____
Beetroot	_____
Beer (8 fluid oz)	_____
Coconut	_____
Coffee (8 fluid oz)	_____
Spirits (1.5 fluid oz)	_____
Oatmeal	_____

Pecans	_____
Tea (8 fluid oz brewed 5 minutes or less)	_____
Walnuts	_____
Wheat germ	_____
Total (add column)	_____ (L)

DIVIDE the total number of servings (L) of Calcium
Henchmen by 4 and write your answer here   _____ (M)
This total is your number of points from *Calcium Henchmen.*

Write your *Calcium Henchmen* points here   _____ (M)
Write your *Calcium Villains* points here   _____ (K)

ADD (M) and (K) and write the total here   _____ (N)
    This is your total points from *Calcium Robbers*

Calcium Score Sheet

Write total points from *Calcium Foods* here   _____ (I)
Write total points from *Calcium Robbers* here   _____ (N)
SUBTRACT N from I and write answer here   _____ (T)
    This is your *Total Calcium Score.*

Interpreting your *Total Calcium Score.*

If your score is:	Your estimated calcium intake in milligrams per day is:	Your calcium range in milligrams is:	Your calcium intake is:
Less than 5	Less than 50	0 to 100	Seriously low
5 to 14	100	90 to 200	Seriously low
15 to 24	200	189 to 390	Seriously low
25 to 34	300	280 to 590	Seriously low
35 to 44	400	370 to 780	Seriously low
45 to 54	500	460 to 980	Seriously low
55 to 64	600	550 to 1,180	Low
65 to 74	700	640 to 1,370	Low

75 to 84	800	740 to 1,570	May be adequate
85 to 94	900	830 to 1,760	May be adequate
95 to 104	1,000	920 to 1,960	May be adequate
105 to 114	1,100	1,010 to 2,160	May be adequate
115+	1,200+	1,100 to 2,350	May be adequate

Please see chart on page 85 to check your calcium need according to your sex, age and region.

PART TWO

THE CALCIUM DIET PROGRAMME

CHAPTER EIGHT

THE CALCIUM DIET

Weight maintenance, even weight loss, can go hand in hand with the dietary principles we recommend. This chapter presents you with *two* complete diets high in both calcium and vitamin D – one for women of 2,000 calories a day, and one for men with 2,700 calories. These amounts should permit moderately active men and women to increase their calcium level to a satisfactory level, while maintaining a normal weight.

If you wish to lose weight, Chapter 9 contains a 1,200-calorie diet rich in calcium that will help you to lose weight. The weight-loss diet should be followed for no longer than two months at a time.

If you wish to design your own diet, you can use Tables 8.1 and 8.2. These give the daily intakes of calcium and vitamin D which we feel are needed to cut your risk of the calcium-deficiency diseases discussed in this book, including breast and colon cancer. The amounts recommended are similar to those of the American National Academy of Sciences, with additional amounts for regions with low levels of ultraviolet light, and for older people.

The proper calcium and vitamin D intake for you depends on where you live and your lifestyle. The main factor you need to know to make the proper choice is your Total Vitamin D Score from your profile in Chapter 7. Look back on page 75 and see what your score is, then use the tables to select the right amount of vitamin D and calcium for you. For a quick idea of which amounts are right for you, use the diet zone map on page 74 of the profile to determine your ultraviolet light level; then use these tables to choose your desirable vitamin D and calcium level.

The usable calcium content of most common foods is shown in the Calcium Counter of Absorbable (Usable) Calcium (Appendix A). Only a few foods contain significant amounts of vitamin D. Many ocean foods such as shark, sole, halibut, cod and shellfish which you might expect to contain vitamin D, unfortunately contain very little. The vitamin D content of the principal foods containing vitamin D is listed in Table 8.3 on page 87.

Instructions: The tables tell you how much calcium you need each day according to where you live, your sex, age, and other factors.

The Diets

Each diet lasts for twenty-eight days. Both contain 60 per cent complex carbohydrates, 20 per cent protein, and 20 per cent fat, including a large amount of omega-3 fish oils. Omega-3 fish oils have been shown to lower cholesterol in the blood and to reduce risk of arteriosclerosis. A chart at the back of the diet plan lists the calcium and calories in each food in the plan.

Breakfast each day includes a tofu shake, a drink that typifies the high-calcium, low-calorie, low-fat foods we recommend. Weekday lunches are simple and portable for eating away from home. Preparation of the weekday meals requires only about fifteen minutes. Weekend meals are designed for greater leisure time and may require longer preparation.

Table 8.1. Desirable daily intakes of calcium (in milligrams) to prevent calcium deficiency diseases (high-risk groups, ages 19+ years: add 200 mg).*

	Your zone score				
	0–1	2	3	4–5	6–7
	Men				
Age	Desirable daily calcium intake (mg)				
Birth to 6 months	360	360	360	360	360
6 months to a year	540	540	540	540	540
1–10 years	800	800	800	800	800
11–18 years	1,200	1,200	1,200	1,200	1,200
19–49 years	1,000	1,000	1,000	800	800
50–59 years	1,000	1,000	1,000	800	800
60–64 years	1,000	1,000	1,000	1,000	800
65+ years	1,000	1,000	1,000	1,000	800
	Women				
Age	Desirable daily calcium intake (mg)				
Birth to 6 months	360	360	360	360	360
6 months to a year	540	540	540	540	540
1–5 years	800	800	800	800	800
6–10 years	950	950	950	900	800
11–18 years	1,200	1,200	1,200	1,200	1,200
19–49 years	1,200	1,200	1,000	800	800
50–59 years	1,500†	1,500†	1,500†	1,250†	1,000
60–64 years	1,500†	1,500†	1,500†	1,250†	1,000
65+ years	1,200	1,200	1,200	1,000	1,000

Pregnant or breast-feeding women, any age: add 300 mg per day

Always drink 2.5 quarts of fluids a day, more when it is hot or you are perspiring. You must produce a urinary volume of 2 quarts a day. Keep dietary oxalate below 50 mg a day (see Appendix E). The information in the first table is based on the authors' research.

High-risk groups include: heavy drinkers, people taking medications that reduce calcium absorption, and night workers. Do not add if you are already adding 300 mg for pregnancy or breast feeding. Never exceed 2,000 mg intake of calcium per day unless under the advice and supervision of a doctor.
† 1,200 milligrams in women receiving replacement oestrogens.

Table 8.2. Desirable daily intakes of vitamin D (in international units) to prevent calcium deficiency diseases (high-risk groups, ages 23 + years: Add 100 I U).†

	Your zone score				
	0–1	2	3	4–5	6–7
	Men				
Age	*Desirable daily vitamin D intake (IU)*				
Birth to 18 years	400	400	400	400	400
19–22 years	400	400	350	300	300
23–64 years	400	200	200	200	200
65–69 years	400	210	200	200	200
70–79 years	400	220	210	200	200
80–84 years	400	230	220	200	200
85 + years	400	240	230	200	200
	Women				
Age	*Desirable daily vitamin D intake (IU)*				
Birth to 18 years	400	400	400	400	400
19–22 years	400	400	400	400	300
23–49 years	400	400	400	400	200
50–69 years	400	400	400	400	200
70–79 years	400	400	400	400	200
80–84 years	400	400	400	400	200
85 + years	400	300	300	300	200

Pregnant or breast-feeding women, zone score 6–7 only, any age: Add 200 I U

† *Always drink 2.5 quarts of fluids a day, more when it is hot or you are perspiring.* If you are ill or have a personal family history of kidney stones, do not modify your intake of vitamin D except on the advice of a health professional.

High-risk groups include: heavy drinkers, people taking medications that reduce calcium absorption, and night workers. Do not add the 100 I U if already adding 200 I U for pregnancy or breast feeding.

Table 8.3. Vitamin D Content of the Principal Vitamin-D-containing Foods *

Food	Vitamin D (IU per 100 gram serving)†
Butter, 2 pats	10
Catfish	2,000
Cheese	10
Cod liver oil, tablespoon	1,175
Eel	4,700
Egg (1)	35
Flounder	40
Herring, canned	135
Herring, fresh	900
Liver, beef	25
Liver, chicken	50
Low-fat spreads, fortified	85
Mackerel	700
Margarine	85
Milk (8 oz)‡	3
Milk, evaporated	112
Pilchard	320
Salmon, Atlantic	1
Salmon, Pacific	500
Sardines, fresh	1,500
Sardines, not in oil	300
Sardines, canned in oil	10
Tuna, canned	215

*The abbreviation IU stands for international units. One international unit is equivalent to 0.025 micrograms of vitamin D3.
† Except as specified for selected foods.
‡ If fortified with vitamin D, milk generally contains 100 IU per 8 oz.
Sources: Paul A. A., Southgate D. A. T. McCance and Widdowson's *Composition of Foods*, 4th ed., HMSO, except dairy products, which are from the National Dairy Council.

The cornerstone tofu shake is easily prepared in the blender from milk, fruit and tofu. Tofu, also known as soybean curd or cake, is usually associated with oriental food. Since it is low in calories and often high in calcium, it is worthy of an important role in many recipes. You will meet it often and, we hope, pleasurably in *The Calcium Diet*. (At the health food shop you will probably find tofu with the cheeses.)

To make as much as possible of the diet's calcium available for absorption by your body, we strongly recommend that you include fruits that are low in calcium-robbing oxalates. The following table lists the fruits we recommend. (Appendix E gives more information about the oxalate content of different foods.)

Low-oxalate Fruits
Apples
Apricots
Bananas
Cherries
Grapefruit
Mangoes
Melons
Nectarines
Oranges
Peaches
Pears
Pineapple
White grapes

Use fresh fruits and vegetables whenever possible. If you use frozen fruits, purchase unsweetened brands. Weekday lunches can be a special problem, since many people depend on fast-food restaurants for lunch. We have found that several of the items commonly available at fast-food restaurants fulfil our dietary recommendations, and we have included them. We have suggested one glass of wine with dinner. If you don't drink alcohol, drink a glass of fruit juice or skimmed milk instead.

Drink a total of eight to ten eight-ounce glasses of fluid a day. The water you drink should contain at least 30 milligrams of calcium per pint. Some municipal water provides this. (Consult Appendix B at the back of the book for a list of the calcium content of the water provided by your local water authority.) If your municipal water supply does not contain 50 milligrams of calcium per quart, Evian is one of the spring or bottled waters with high amounts of calcium you may want to use instead. Daily, you must also take one of the multiple vitamin and mineral supplements that provide 100 per cent of the recommended daily allowance (RDA) of vitamins and minerals. You will not need a calcium supplement.

A different menu is presented for each day – no two days are alike. An asterisk (*) next to a food means that a recipe for it is given in Part III. If no food portion or amount is listed, it means that a standard portion is intended. 'Milk' means skimmed milk or buttermilk, eight ounces. We assume eight-ounce portions of juice and herb tea also. 'Wine' refers to six ounces of table or vintage wine, not fortified wines such as sherry or port.

For vegetables, 'hot' means steamed. Bread or toast assumes two slices, from loaves made from enriched white flour. Sandwiches may have enriched white, French, pita or sourdough bread. 'Oil' means olive oil, one tablespoon. 'Lemon juice' also means one tablespoonful. Where other fats are called for, one teaspoon is implied. Dressings assume one tablespoonful.

These diets contain 800 milligrams of calcium. If your desirable intake is 1,000 to 1,200 milligrams, then add high-calcium foods to your diet. An additional glass of skimmed milk will boost your calcium intake to over 1,000 milligrams a day – while adding only 90 calories.

THE 2,000 CALORIE DIET FOR WOMEN

DAY 1/MONDAY/WEEK 1

BREAKFAST
★Tofu shake
Raisin toast with butter

SNACK
Fruit
Citrus juice

LUNCH
Mixed vegetable sandwich
Fruit
Milk (6 ounces)

SNACK
Apple juice

DINNER
★Chicken casserole
Cucumber slices with
    lemon juice
Hot rice (2 servings)
Wine
★Citrus sorbet

SNACK
Apple juice

DAY 2/TUESDAY/WEEK 1

BREAKFAST
★Tofu shake

SNACK
Fruit (2 servings)
Milk

LUNCH
Green salad with french
    dressing
Roll
Milk

SNACK
Citrus juice
Fruit

DINNER
★Vermicelli with sauce
Sliced cucumber with oil
    and vinegar
Wine
★Citrus sorbet

SNACK
Fruit

DAY 3/WEDNESDAY/WEEK 1

BREAKFAST
* Tofu shake

SNACK
Citrus juice

LUNCH
Turkey breast and tomato
  sandwich
Salad with french dressing
Milk
Fruit

DINNER
* Halibut steak with capers
* Mushrooms and pasta
Lettuce with lemon juice
Wine
Citrus sorbet

SNACK
Fruit

DAY 4/THURSDAY/WEEK 1

BREAKFAST
* Tofu shake

SNACK
Wholemeal roll with
  butter
Citrus juice

LUNCH
Salad
Fruit

DINNER
* Fettuccine with tomatoes
  and parmesan cheese
Sliced mushrooms and
  cucumber with oil,
  lemon juice and herbs
Roll
Wine
* Citrus sorbet

DAY 5/FRIDAY/WEEK 1

BREAKFAST
* Tofu shake
Toast with butter,
  cinnamon and fructose

SNACK
Egg salad sandwich
Milk (4 ounces)
Fruit (2 servings)

DINNER
* Caesar salad
Roll with butter
Wine
* Pears in wine

SNACK
Fruit
* Poppyseed dressing

DAY 6/SATURDAY/WEEK 1

BREAKFAST
* Tofu shake
Toast with butter and jam

LUNCH
Fruit salad
* Poppyseed dressing
Rolls (2)
Citrus juice

SNACK
Apple juice

DINNER
* Seafood strata
Lettuce, tomato and
  cucumber with oil
  (1 teaspoon), vinegar
  and herbs
* Fresh fruit sorbet (1½
  servings)

SNACK
Fruit

DAY 7/SUNDAY/WEEK 1

BREAKFAST
★ Tofu shake

SNACK
Apple juice

LUNCH
★ Chef's salad (low
    calcium)
Milk (6 ounces)
★ Apple crumble

SNACK
Citrus juice

DINNER
★ Pizza
Sliced cucumber with oil
    and vinegar
Wine
★ Citrus sorbet (2 servings)

DAY 8/MONDAY/WEEK 2

BREAKFAST
★ Tofu shake
Crumpets with jam and
    butter

SNACK
Citrus juice

LUNCH
Mixed vegetable sandwich
Milk (4 ounces)
Fruit
★ Poppyseed dressing

DINNER
★ Vegetable loaves
Sweetcorn with butter
    (2 servings)
Butterhead lettuce,
    tomatoes and
    mushrooms with oil (1
    teaspoon), vinegar and
    herbs
Wine
★ Citrus sorbet

SNACK
Fruit

DAY 9/TUESDAY/WEEK 2

BREAKFAST
*Tofu shake
Wholemeal roll with
   butter

SNACK
Fruit
Citrus juice

LUNCH
Green salad with french
   dressing
Chicken salad sandwich
Fruit (2 servings)

DINNER
*Salmon loaf
Hot baby new potatoes
   and peas tossed with oil,
   vinegar and herbs
Wine
*Peach bake

SNACK
Apple juice

DAY 10/WEDNESDAY/WEEK 2

BREAKFAST
*Tofu shake
Crumpets with butter and
   jam

SNACK
Fruit

LUNCH
Mixed vegetable sandwich
Fruit

DINNER
*Spaghetti with
   mushrooms and
   tomatoes
Cucumber with oil (2
   tablespoons), lemon
   juice and herbs
Wine
*Citrus sorbet

SNACK
Fruit

DAY 11/THURSDAY/WEEK 2

BREAKFAST
*Tofu shake
Roll

SNACK
Milk
Roll

LUNCH
Green salad with french
　dressing
Citrus juice

DINNER
Chicken breasts grilled
　with oil, lemon juice,
　ginger and rosemary (2
　servings)
Pasta (2 servings) with
　butter
Tomato and cucumber
　with oil and lemon juice
Wine
*Citrus sorbet (2 servings)

SNACK
Fruit

DAY 12/FRIDAY/WEEK 2

BREAKFAST
*Tofu shake

SNACK
Fruit (2 servings)
Milk (6 ounces)

LUNCH
Chicken salad sandwich
Fruit
Citrus fruit

SNACK
Apple juice
Roll

DINNER
*Sea salad
Pasta with butter (2
　servings)
Wine

DAY 13/SATURDAY/WEEK 2

BREAKFAST
★Tofu shake

SNACK
Fruit

LUNCH
Turkey breast and tomato
  sandwich
Milk (4 ounces)
Citrus juice
Fruit (2 servings)

DINNER
★Linguine and broccoli
Wine
★Citrus sorbet

SNACK
Fruit

DAY 14/SUNDAY/WEEK 2

BREAKFAST
★Tofu shake

SNACK
Fruit
Roll with butter

LUNCH
★Vegetable caviar
Bread
Fruit
Milk (4 ounces)

SNACK
Citrus juice

DINNER
★Pasta with corn and ham
Rolls (2) with butter
Wine
Fruit
★Fresh fruit sorbet

DAY 15/MONDAY/WEEK 3

BREAKFAST
* Tofu shake

SNACK
Fruit
Citrus juice

LUNCH
Fruit salad (2 servings)
Roll
Milk

SNACK
Apple juice

DINNER
* Spaghettini and clam
   sauce
Sliced cucumber and
   tomatoes with oil and
   lemon juice
Wine
* Citrus sorbet

DAY 16/TUESDAY/WEEK 3

BREAKFAST
* Tofu shake

SNACK
Fruit
Citrus juice

LUNCH
Pasta salad (2 servings)
Fruit
Milk

SNACK
Apple juice

DINNER
* Chicken kebabs
Hot corn on the cob (2
   servings) with butter
Lettuce with french
   dressing
Wine
* Baked apples

SNACK
Fruit

DAY 17/WEDNESDAY/WEEK 3

BREAKFAST
★Tofu shake

SNACK
Fruit roll
Citrus juice

LUNCH
Chicken salad sandwich
Milk

DINNER
★Trout in wine sauce
Hot baby turnips, pasta
    and carrots with oil,
    lemon juice and herbs
Wine
★Citrus sorbet

DAY 18/THURSDAY/WEEK 3

BREAKFAST
★Tofu shake

SNACK
Milk (4 ounces)

LUNCH
Tuna salad sandwich
Green salad with garlic
    dressing
Citrus juice

DINNER
★Pasta with cabbage and
    scallions
Cherry tomatoes and
    mushroom slices with
    lemon juice and herbs
Wine
★Citrus sorbet

SNACK
Apple juice

DAY 19/FRIDAY/WEEK 3

BREAKFAST
★ Tofu shake

SNACK
Fruit
Fruit muffin or fruit cake
Milk

LUNCH
Turkey breast and tomato
   sandwich
Citrus juice
Fruit

SNACK
Apple juice

DINNER
★ Sole (baked) (2 servings)
★ Rice pilaf (2 servings)
Cucumber slices with oil
   and lemon juice
Wine
★ Citrus sorbet

DAY 20/SATURDAY/WEEK 3

BREAKFAST
★ Tofu shake
Fruit muffin or fruit cake

LUNCH
Pasta salad
Apple juice

SNACK
★ Citrus sorbet (2 servings)

DINNER
★ Cream of champagne
   soup (half serving)
Hot whole artichoke
★ Mayonnaise
Steamed lobster tails (2
   servings)
Melted butter (1
   tablespoon)
French roll
Champagne
Kiwi and papaya/paw paw
★ Fruit salad dressing (2
   tablespoons)

DAY 21/SUNDAY/WEEK 3

BREAKFAST
* Tofu shake
Raisin bread (1 slice)

LUNCH
* Cheesey scrambled eggs
* Blueberry bun
Milk (6 ounces)
* Poppyseed dressing with fruit

DINNER
Salmon grilled with oil (1 teaspoon), lemon juice and cilantro leaves
Lettuce and tomato salad with lemon juice
Corn muffin or small slice plain cake
Wine
* Citrus sorbet (2 servings)

SNACK
Fruit

DAY 22/MONDAY/WEEK 4

BREAKFAST
* Tofu shake

SNACK
Fruit (2 servings)
Citrus juice

LUNCH
Fruit salad
Corn muffins (2) or slice cake
Milk (6 ounces)

SNACK
Apple juice

DINNER
Grilled chicken breast (2 servings)
Hot baby potatoes and baby peas, tossed with margarine (2 teaspoons) and herbs
Wine
* Peach bake or slice cake

SNACK
Apple juice

DAY 23/TUESDAY/WEEK 4

BREAKFAST
★ Tofu shake

SNACK
Fruit muffin or fruit cake
Fruit

LUNCH
Mixed vegetable sandwich
Fruit
Milk

DINNER
★ Egg salad
Garlic bread with butter (1 slice)
Wine
Fruit
★ Poppyseed dressing

SNACK
★ Citrus sorbet (2 servings)

DAY 24/WEDNESDAY/WEEK 4

BREAKFAST
★ Tofu shake

SNACK
Fruit
Citrus juice

LUNCH
Pasta salad (2 servings)
Roll
Milk
Fruit

SNACK
Apple juice

DINNER
★ Codfish (grilled) (2 servings)
★ Red cabbage
Hot new potatoes
Wine
★ Citrus sorbet

SNACK
Fruit

DAY 25/THURSDAY/WEEK 4

BREAKFAST
★ Tofu shake

SNACK
Fruit
Milk

LUNCH
Salmon salad sandwich
Milk (4 ounces)
Fruit (2 servings)

DINNER
★ Linguine and cauliflower
Wine
★ Citrus sorbet (2 servings)

SNACK
Apple juice

DAY 26/FRIDAY/WEEK 4

BREAKFAST
★ Tofu shake

SNACK
Fruit
Citrus juice

LUNCH
Turkey breast and tomato
    sandwich
Milk (4 ounces)
Fruit (2 servings)

SNACK
Apple juice

DINNER
★ Vegetables with noodles
Wine
★ Citrus sorbet

SNACK
Fruit
★ Poppyseed dressing

DAY 27/SATURDAY/WEEK 4

BREAKFAST
★ Tofu shake
Fruit roll

SNACK
Fruit

LUNCH
Chicken salad sandwich
Milk (4 ounces)
Fruit
★ Poppyseed dressing

SNACK
Apple juice

DINNER
★ Oyster sandwich
Tomato slices
Wine
★ Citrus sorbet

SNACK
Apple juice

DAY 28/SUNDAY/WEEK 4

BREAKFAST
★ Tofu shake

SNACK
Fruit

LUNCH
★ Stuffed eggs
Pasta salad
Milk (4 ounces)

DINNER
★ Tacos
★ Tomato purée (1½ servings)
★ Citrus sorbet (2 servings)
Wine

SNACK
Apple juice

THE 2,700 CALORIE DIET FOR MEN

DAY 1/MONDAY/WEEK 1

BREAKFAST
*Tofu shake
Raisin toast with butter
   and jam
Fruit

SNACK
Citrus juice

LUNCH
Mixed vegetable sandwich
   with mayonnaise
Fruit
Milk

SNACK
Apple juice

DINNER
*Chicken casserole
Hot rice (2 servings)
Cucumber slices with oil,
   lemon juice and herbs
Wine
*Citrus sorbet (2 servings)

SNACK
Fruit
Apple juice

DAY 2/TUESDAY/WEEK 1

BREAKFAST
*Tofu shake
Fruit

SNACK
Fruit
Milk

LUNCH
Green salad with french
   dressing (3 servings)
Roll
Citrus juice

SNACK
Fruit

DINNER
*Vermicelli with tomato
   sauce
Sliced cucumber with oil
   (1 tablespoon), vinegar
   and herbs
Wine
*Citrus sorbet (2 servings)

SNACK
Fruit

DAY 3/WEDNESDAY/WEEK 1

BREAKFAST
*Tofu shake
Toast and jam

SNACK
Citrus juice

LUNCH
Egg salad sandwich
Salad with french dressing
Milk (4 ounces)
Fruit

DINNER
*Halibut steak with capers
*Mushrooms and pasta
Lettuce with lemon juice
    and olive oil (1
    tablespoon)
Wine
*Citrus sorbet (2 servings)

SNACK
Fruit

DAY 4/THURSDAY/WEEK 1

BREAKFAST
*Tofu shake
Wholemeal roll with
    butter

SNACK
Citrus juice

LUNCH
Salmon salad sandwich
Milk (four ounces)
Fruit

SNACK
Apple juice

DINNER
*Fettuccine with tomatoes
    and parmesan cheese
Mushroom and cucumber
    slices with oil (2
    tablespoons), lemon
    juice and herbs
Roll
Wine
*Citrus sorbet (2 servings)

DAY 5/FRIDAY/WEEK 1

BREAKFAST
*Tofu shake
Toast, with butter,
   fructose and cinnamon

SNACK
Citrus juice

LUNCH
Turkey breast and tomato
   sandwich
Fruit (2 servings)

DINNER
*Caesar salad
Rolls with butter (2)
Wine
*Pears in wine (2
   servings)

SNACK
Fruit (2 servings)
*Poppyseed dressing
*Citrus sorbet (2
   tablespoons)

DAY 6/SATURDAY/WEEK 1

BREAKFAST
*Tofu shake
Toast with butter and jam

LUNCH
Fruit salad
*Poppyseed dressing
Fruit rolls (2)
Citrus juice

SNACK
Apple juice

DINNER
*Seafood strata
Lettuce, tomato and
   cucumber with oil (2
   tablespoons), vinegar
   and herbs
Wine
*Citrus sorbet (2 servings)

SNACK
Fruit

DAY 7/SUNDAY/WEEK 1

BREAKFAST
*Tofu shake

SNACK
Apple juice

LUNCH
*Chef's salad (low
    calcium)
Milk (4 ounces)
*Apple crumble (2
    servings)

SNACK
Citrus juice

DINNER
*Pizza
Sliced cucumber with oil,
    vinegar and herbs
Wine
*Citrus sorbet (2 servings)

DAY 8/MONDAY/WEEK 2

BREAKFAST
*Tofu shake
Crumpets with jam and
    butter

SNACK
Citrus juice

LUNCH
Mixed vegetable sandwich
    with dressing
Fruit (2 servings)
*Poppyseed dressing (2
    tablespoons)

SNACK
Fruit

DINNER
*Vegetable loaves
Sweetcorn with butter (2
    servings)
Lettuce, tomato wedges
    and sliced mushrooms
    with oil (2 tablespoons),
    vinegar and herbs
Wine
*Citrus sorbet (2 servings)

SNACK
Apple juice

DAY 9/TUESDAY/WEEK 2

BREAKFAST
*Tofu shake
Wholemeal roll with
    butter and jam (1
    tablespoon)
Fruit

SNACK
Citrus juice
Cinnamon roll

LUNCH
Green salad with french
    dressing (2 servings)
Chicken salad sandwich
Fruit (2 servings)

DINNER
*Salmon loaf
Hot baby new potatoes
    and baby peas tossed
    with oil, vinegar and
    herbs
Wine
*Peach bake

SNACK
*Citrus sorbet (2 servings)

DAY 10/WEDNESDAY/WEEK 2

BREAKFAST
*Tofu shake
Crumpets with butter and
    jam

SNACK
Fruit (2 servings)

LUNCH
Mixed vegetable sandwich
    (2)
Fruit
Apple juice

DINNER
*Spaghetti bolognese
Cucumber with oil (2
    tablespoons), lemon
    juice and herbs
Wine
*Citrus sorbet (2 servings)

DAY 11/THURSDAY/WEEK 2

BREAKFAST
* Tofu shake
Roll

SNACK
Roll
Citrus juice

LUNCH
Green salad with french
  dressing (2 servings)
Tuna salad sandwich
Milk

DINNER
Chicken breasts grilled
  with oil, lemon juice,
  ginger and rosemary
Pasta (2 servings)
Tomato and cucumber
  with oil (1 tablespoon),
  vinegar and herbs
Wine
* Citrus sorbet (2 servings)

SNACK
Fruit

DAY 12/FRIDAY/WEEK 2

BREAKFAST
* Tofu shake
Fruit (2 servings)

SNACK
Milk (4 ounces)
Fruit

LUNCH
Chicken salad sandwich
  with dressing
Fruit
Citrus juice

SNACK
Apple juice
Fruit roll

DINNER
* Sea salad (1½ servings)
Pasta with olive oil (2
  servings)
Wine
* Citrus sorbet (2 servings)

SNACK
Apple juice

DAY 13/SATURDAY/WEEK 2

BREAKFAST
★ Tofu shake
Fruit

SNACK
Apple juice

LUNCH
Turkey breast and tomato
  sandwich (2)
Fruit with dressing (2
  servings)

SNACK
Citrus juice

DINNER
★ Linguine and broccoli
Wine
★ Citrus sorbet (2
  servings)

DAY 14/SUNDAY/WEEK 2

BREAKFAST
★ Tofu shake
Fruit
Roll with butter

LUNCH
★ Vegetable caviar
Bread
Fruit
Milk (4 ounces)

SNACK
Citrus juice

DINNER
★ Pasta with corn and ham
Rolls with butter (2)
Wine
★ Citrus sorbet (2 servings)

SNACK
Apple juice

DAY 15/MONDAY/WEEK 3

BREAKFAST
★ Tofu shake
Fruit

SNACK
Citrus juice

LUNCH
Fruit salad with apple (2
    servings)
Roll
Milk

SNACK
Apple juice

DINNER
★ Spaghettini with clam
    sauce
Butterhead or other
    lettuce, cucumber and
    tomato with oil (2
    tablespoons), lemon
    juice and herbs
Milk
★ Citrus sorbet (2 servings)

SNACK
Apple juice

DAY 16/TUESDAY/WEEK 3

BREAKFAST
★ Tofu shake
Fruit

SNACK
Citrus juice

LUNCH
Pasta salad (2 servings)
Fruit
Milk (6 ounces)

SNACK
Apple juice

DINNER
★ Chicken kebabs
Hot corn on the cob with
    butter (2 servings)
Green salad with french
    dressing
Wine
★ Baked apples (2 servings)

SNACK
★ Citrus sorbet (2 servings)

DAY 17/WEDNESDAY/WEEK 3

BREAKFAST
★ Tofu shake
Fruit

SNACK
Fruit roll with jam
Citrus juice

LUNCH
Chicken salad sandwich
Fruit
Milk (4 ounces)

SNACK
Apple juice

DINNER
★ Trout in wine sauce
Hot baby turnips, baby
    carrots and cooked pasta
    with oil (2 tablespoons),
    lemon juice and herbs
Wine
★ Citrus sorbet (2 servings)

SNACK
Fruit

DAY 18/THURSDAY/WEEK 3

BREAKFAST
★ Tofu shake
Fruit

SNACK
Cinnamon roll

LUNCH
Tuna salad sandwich
Green salad with garlic
    dressing
Fruit
Citrus juice

DINNER
★ Pasta with cabbage and
    scallions ($1\frac{1}{2}$ servings)
Sliced tomato and
    mushrooms with lemon
    juice, oil (1 tablespoon)
    and herbs
Wine
★ Citrus sorbet (2 servings)

SNACK
Apple juice

DAY 19/FRIDAY/WEEK 3

BREAKFAST
*Tofu shake
Fruit

SNACK
Fruit muffin or plain cake
with jam
Milk

LUNCH
Turkey breast and tomato
sandwich with dressing
Citrus juice
Fruit

SNACK
Apple juice

DINNER
*Sole (baked) (2 servings)
*Rice pilaf (2 servings)
Cucumber slices with oil
(1 tablespoon), lemon
juice and herbs
Wine
*Citrus sorbet (2 servings)

SNACK
Apple juice

DAY 20/SATURDAY/WEEK 3

BREAKFAST
*Tofu shake
Fruit muffins (2) or plain
cake with jam

LUNCH
Pasta salad (2 servings)
Apple juice
*Citrus sorbet

DINNER
*Cream of champagne
soup (half serving)
Hot whole artichoke
*Mayonnaise

Steamed lobster tails (2
servings)
Melted butter (2
tablespoons)
French roll
Champagne
Kiwi and papaya/paw paw
*Fruit salad dressing (2
tablespoons)

SNACK
Apple juice
*Citrus sorbet

DAY 21/SUNDAY/WEEK 3

BREAKFAST
*Tofu shake
Raisin toast and jam
Fruit

SNACK
Apple juice

LUNCH
*Cheesey scrambled eggs
*Blueberry bun
Fruit
*Poppyseed dressing (1
  tablespoon)
Citrus juice

SNACK
Apple juice

DINNER
Salmon grilled with oil (1
  tablespoon), lemon juice
  and parsley
Lettuce and tomato with
  oil (2 tablespoons),
  lemon juice and herbs
Roll
Wine
*Citrus sorbet (2 servings)

SNACK
Fruit

DAY 22/MONDAY/WEEK 4

BREAKFAST
*Tofu shake
Fruit (2 servings)

SNACK
Citrus juice

LUNCH
Fruit salad (2 servings)
Rolls (2)
Milk (6 ounces)

SNACK
Apple juice

DINNER
Broiled chicken breast (2
  servings)
Hot baby new potatoes
  and baby peas, tossed
  with butter (2
  teaspoons) and herbs
Wine
*Peach bake (2 servings)

SNACK
*Citrus sorbet (2 servings)

DAY 23/TUESDAY/WEEK 4

BREAKFAST
*Tofu shake
Fruit

SNACK
Fruit muffin or cake
Citrus juice

LUNCH
Mixed vegetable sandwich
  (2) with dressing
Fruit
Milk (4 ounces)

DINNER
*Egg salad
Garlic bread with olive oil
  (2 servings)
Wine
Fruit
*Poppyseed dressing

SNACK
*Citrus sorbet (2 servings)

DAY 24/WEDNESDAY/WEEK 4

BREAKFAST
*Tofu shake
Fruit

SNACK
Citrus juice

LUNCH
Pasta salad (2 servings)
Roll with jam
Green salad with garlic
  dressing (2 tablespoons)
Milk
Fruit

SNACK
Apple juice

DINNER
*Codfish (grilled) (2
  servings)
*Red cabbage
Hot new potatoes
Wine
*Citrus sorbet (2 servings)

SNACK
Fruit

DAY 25/THURSDAY/WEEK 4

BREAKFAST
★Tofu shake
Fruit

SNACK
Fruit (2 servings)

LUNCH
Salmon salad sandwich
Mixed salad with french
    dressing (2 servings)
Milk (4 ounces)
Fruit (2 servings)

SNACK
Apple juice

DINNER
★Linguine and cauliflower
Wine
★Citrus sorbet (2 servings)

SNACK
Apple juice

DAY 26/FRIDAY/WEEK 4

BREAKFAST
★Tofu shake
Fruit

SNACK
Citrus juice

LUNCH
Turkey breast and tomato
    sandwich with dressing
Milk
Fruit (2 servings)

SNACK
Apple juice

DINNER
★Vegetables with noodles
Wine
Fruit
★Poppyseed dressing

SNACK
★Citrus sorbet (2 servings)
Apple juice

DAY 27/SATURDAY/WEEK 4

BREAKFAST
⋆ Tofu shake
Fruit roll

SNACK
Fruit

LUNCH
Chicken salad sandwich
    with dressing
Fruit (2 servings)
⋆ Poppyseed dressing (2
    servings)
Milk (4 ounces)

SNACK
Apple juice

DINNER
⋆ Oyster sandwich
Tomato slices with olive
    oil (1 tablespoon) and
    vinegar
Wine
⋆ Citrus sorbet (2 servings)

SNACK
Apple juice

DAY 28/SUNDAY/WEEK 4

BREAKFAST
⋆ Tofu shake
Fruit

SNACK
Apple juice

LUNCH
⋆ Stuffed eggs
Pasta salad (3 servings)
Lettuce with oil (1
    tablespoon) and lemon
    juice
Milk (4 ounces)

DINNER
⋆ Tacos
⋆ Tomato purée (2
    servings)
Green salad with oil (1
    tablespoon) and vinegar
Wine
⋆ Citrus sorbet (2 servings)

SNACK
Apple juice

Table 8.4. Shows the calcium-to-calorie ratio of basic foods and dishes mentioned in the diets in this chapter and Chapter 5.

Table 8.4
CALCIUM-CALORIE RATIO

One serving is generally considered 3.5 ounces, though serving sizes may vary according to the recipe.

Food/Recipe per serving	Calcium (mg)	Calories	Ca/Cal ratio	Diets with *recipes 2 000/ 2 700 cal	1 200 cal
Yogurt (3.5 oz)	190	50	3.8		
Kale (3.5 oz)	178	53	3.4		
Skim milk (8-oz glass)	271	81	3.3		
Broccoli (3.5 oz)	103	32	3.2		
Parmesan cheese (3.5 oz)	1,140	393	2.9		
*Anchovy spread	196	75	2.6	√	
Grapefruit (3.5 oz)	41	16	2.6		
Swiss cheese (3.5 oz)	925	370	2.5		
Butterhead lettuce (3.5 oz)	35	14	2.5		
*Anchovy spread (high calcium)	273	118	2.3		
Sardines, canned with tomato sauce (3.5 oz)	449	197	2.3		
*Vegetable-yogurt loaf (high calcium)	504	220	2.3		
*Cream of champagne soup	531	241	2.2	√	√
Cabbage (3.5 oz)	49	24	2.0		
Artichoke (3.5 oz)	51	25	2.0		
*Vegetable-yogurt loaf	186	97	1.9	√	
Cheddar cheese (3.5 oz)	750	398	1.9		
Tofu (3.5 oz)	128	72	1.8		
*Vegetable caviar (high calcium)	300	172	1.7		
*Tofu shake	228	136	1.7	√	√
Cucumber (3.5 oz)	25	15	1.7		
*Cauliflower with crab	98	62	1.6		

Table 8.4 – *continued*

Food/Recipe per serving	Calcium (mg)	Calories	Ca/Cal ratio	Diets with * recipes	
				2 000/ 2 700 cal	1 200 cal
*Broccoli with cheese sauce	233	142	1.6		√
*Seafood strata with cheese	940	609	1.5		
*Salmon mould	367	241	1.5		√
*Baked broccoli	175	116	1.5		√
*Salmon loaf	310	208	1.5	√	√
Eastern oysters (3.5 oz)	94	66	1.4		
Omelette with tofu and cheese (high calcium)	293	210	1.4		
*Salmon bake (high calcium)	634	448	1.4		
*Pasta with mushrooms, pimiento and cheese (high calcium)	519	365	1.4		
*Tacos (high calcium)	655	465	1.4		
*Cheese log	404	287	1.4		√
*Salmon bake	448	335	1.3		√
*Mayonnaise	49	37	1.3	√	√
*Caesar salad (high calcium)	401	316	1.3		
*Vegetable loaves	201	166	1.2	√	
*Tuna fillets in wine	328	274	1.2		
*Broccoli (baked) (high calcium)	229	194	1.2		
*Gourmet cheese dressing (1 tablespoon)	53	47	1.1		√
*Chef's salad (high calcium)	457	412	1.1		
*Vegetable caviar	97	90	1.1	√	√
Salmon	180	170	1.1		
*Cheese dip	123	129	1.0		
*Courgette and mushroom salad	86	84	1.0		
*Pasta shells with tomato sauce	487	498	1.0		√

Table 8.4 – *continued*

Food/Recipe per serving	Calcium (mg)	Calories	Ca/Cal ratio	Diets with *recipes 2 000/ 2 700 cal	1 200 cal
*Seafood strata	356	373	1.0	√	
*Salmon (grilled)	227	238	1.0		√
*Lasagne (high calcium)	779	825	0.9		√
Ricotta cheese (3.5 oz)	160	170	0.9		
*Stuffed eggs	128	139	0.9	√	√
*Chicken cheddar casserole	406	444	0.9		
*Red cabbage	66	73	0.9	√	√
*Cauliflower (3.5 oz)	24	27	0.9		
Cottage cheese (3.5 oz)	94	106	0.9		
*Red snapper with vegetables	172	194	0.9		
*Oysters (grilled, high calcium)	221	249	0.9		
*Cheesey scrambled eggs (high calcium)	178	193	0.9		
*Lasagne with parmesan cheese	652	800	0.8		
*Pasta with mushrooms, pimiento and cheese	294	352	0.8		√
Orange (3.5 oz)	40	49	0.8		
*Fruit parfait	139	172	0.8		
*Ravioli	391	487	0.8		√
*Chef's salad (medium calcium)	265	337	0.8		√
*Chicken casserole (high calcium)	119	158	0.8		√
*Pasta with garden vegetables	144	220	0.7		
*Tacos	203	287	0.7	√	
Shrimp (3.5 oz)	63	91	0.7		
*Linguine and broccoli (low calorie)	268	392	0.7		√
*Broccoli soup	154	221	0.7		

Table 8.4 – *continued*

Food/Recipe per serving	*Calcium (mg)*	*Calories*	*Ca/Cal ratio*	*Diets with * recipes* 2 000/ 2 700 cal	*1 200 cal*
* Omelette with tofu and cheese	127	188	0.7		√
* Scallops in yogurt	94	141	0.7		√
* Shrimp in tomato beds	214	313	0.7		
* Fruit salad dressing (1 tablespoon)	17	31	0.7	√	√
* Shrimp with dill	139	217	0.6		√
* Pasta with broccoli	273	488	0.6		
* Sea salad	106	170	0.6	√	√
* Oysters (grilled)	138	222	0.6		√
* Caesar salad	139	226	0.6	√	√
* Chicken kebabs	148	242	0.6	√	√
* Chicken in parmesan cheese	168	259	0.6		
Tomato (3.5 oz)	13	22	0.6		
* Lasagne	406	702	0.6		√
* Fettuccine with tofu	161	315	0.5		√
* Whipped delight	63	115	0.5		
* Pasta and cheese	407	789	0.5		
* Chef's salad (low calcium)	144	294	0.5	√	
* Chicken in yogurt	123	252	0.5		√
* Turnips with tomatoes	134	277	0.5		
* Oyster sandwich	171	354	0.5	√	
* Tofu croquettes	141	295	0.5		
* Compote of apple	56	119	0.5		√
* Chick peas (celery and onions)	213	458	0.5		
Crab (3.5 oz)	43	93	0.5		
* Shrimp dip	78	169	0.5		√
* Codfish (baked)	169	368	0.5		
* Sauce ricotta	187	445	0.4		
* Linguine and broccoli	283	689	0.4	√	
* Pizza	221	516	0.4	√	

Table 8.4 – *continued*

Food/Recipe per serving	Calcium (mg)	Calories	Ca/Cal ratio	Diets with * recipes	
				2 000/ 2 700 cal	1 200 cal
Plums, damson (3.5 oz)	26	66	0.4		
*Fettuccine with tomatoes and romano cheese	247	681	0.4		
*Spaghetti bolognese	206	569	0.4	√	
*Chicken casserole	48	134	0.4	√	
*Cheesey scrambled eggs	41	116	0.4	√	√
*Shrimp barbecue	173	495	0.3		
*Vermicelli with tomato and cheese sauce	217	650	0.3		
Egg (3.5 oz)	54	163	0.3		
Scallops (3.5 oz)	26	81	0.3		
Lobster (3.5 oz)	29	91	0.3		
*Tomato purée	34	110	0.3	√	
*Vegetables with noodles	186	633	0.3	√	
*Cherry sauce with sorbet	108	344	0.3		√
*Linguine and cauliflower	155	562	0.3	√	
Watermelon (3.5 oz)	7	26	0.3		
*Poppyseed dressing	11	41	0.3	√	√
*Trout in wine sauce	72	275	0.3	√	
*Shrimp with pasta	96	391	0.2		√
Blueberries (3.5 oz)	15	62	0.2		
Peach (3.5 oz)	9	38	0.2		
*Oyster and cod bake	95	474	0.2		
*Fruit sorbet	24	122	0.2		√
*Blackberry pudding	58	301	0.2		
*Pasta with cabbage and scallions	94	493	0.2	√	
Rainbow trout (3.5 oz)	36	195	0.2		
*Blueberry buns	45	271	0.2	√	
*Egg salad	62	375	0.2	√	

Table 8.4 – *continued*

Food/Recipe per serving	Calcium (mg)	Calories	Ca/Cal ratio	Diets with *recipes	
				2 000/ 2 700 cal	1 200 cal
White grapes (3.5 oz)	11	67	0.2		
*Pears in wine	39	238	0.2	√	
*Fettuccine with tomatoes and parmesan cheese	85	537	0.2	√	
*Codfish (grilled)	15	95	0.2	√	√
*Strawberry mould	29	191	0.2		
French bread (3.5 oz)	26	177	0.1		
Albacore (tuna) (3.5 oz)	26	177	0.1		
Atlantic salmon	29	197	0.1		
*Fresh fruit	80	575	0.1		
*Spaghettini with clam sauce	80	580	0.1	√	
*Halibut steak with capers	16	124	0.1	√	
*Fresh fruit sorbet	33	256	0.1	√	
Canned tuna (3.5 oz)	16	127	0.1		
*Vermicelli with tomato sauce	74	601	0.1	√	
Apple (3.5 oz)	7	58	0.1		
Pear (3.5 oz)	7	61	0.1		
Chicken breast (3.5 oz)	11	101	0.1		
White wine (3.5 oz)	9	85	0.1		
Grilled white fish	15	143	0.1		
Applesauce, unsweetened (3.5 oz)	57	587	0.1	√	
*Mushrooms and pasta	57	587	0.1	√	
*Baked apples	22	228	0.1	√	
Banana (3.5 oz)	8	85	0.1		
*Sole (baked)	14	152	0.1	√	
*Apple-cranberry mould	15	164	0.1		
*Rice pilaf	8	90	0.1	√	√
*Pasta with corn and ham	29	339	0.1	√	

Table 8.4 – *continued*

Food/Recipe per serving	Calcium (mg)	Calories	Ca/Cal ratio	Diets with * recipes	
				2 000/ 2 700 cal	1 200 cal
*Peaches in honey	23	307	0.1		
Pasta (3.5 oz)	11	148	0.1		
*Peach bake	21	283	0.1	✓	✓
Nectarine (3.5 oz)	4	64	0.1		
*Bananas (stewed)	17	281	0.1		✓
*Apple crumble	18	299	0.1	✓	
*Citrus sorbet	7	297	0.0	✓	✓

*See Recipe section for all foods marked with an asterisk.

CHAPTER NINE

THE LOW-CALORIE CALCIUM DIET

The following is a high-calcium, *low-calorie* diet especially for people who want to increase their calcium intake but also want to lose weight. The diet runs for thirty days, and you may repeat the cycle. However, we recommend using it for no longer than two months at a time. The diet contains 60 per cent complex carbohydrates, 20 per cent protein, and 20 per cent fat, including a large amount of omega-3 fish oils. Be sure to take a daily multiple vitamin and mineral supplement.

The diet begins at the weekend, with two 'cleansing days' of delicious but extra-low-calories foods, emphasizing fruits and fluids. For the remaining twenty-eight days the daily plan limits your food intake to 1,200 calories. In general the diet follows the same principles found in the regular Calcium Diet in Chapter 8. We do not advise following a weight loss diet during acute illnesses.

The cornerstone of the diet is our own special Tofu milkshake, easily prepared in the blender from milk, fruit and tofu.

In general, we suggest no substitutions in the plan. However, if necessary, the foods in each of the following groupings *are* interchangeable:

oranges, bananas, grapes
grapefruit, pears, apples, plums, peaches, nectarines
skim milk, buttermilk

If necessary, after the first two 'cleansing' days, you may nibble up to four ounces of the following raw vegetables to satisfy any between-meal hunger pains: cucumber, broccoli, carrots, celery or cauliflower.

A different menu is presented for each day – no two days are alike. An asterisk (*) next to a dish means that a recipe for it is given in Part III. You are allowed one serving of each dish – sorry, no seconds. If no amount of food is listed, it means that a standard three-and-one-half-ounce portion is intended. 'Milk' means skimmed milk or buttermilk, eight ounces. We assume eight-ounce measures of juice and herb tea also. 'Wine' means six ounces of table or vintage wine, not fortified wines such as sherry or port. For vegetables, 'hot' means steamed.

DAY 1/FIRST CLEANSING DAY/SATURDAY

BREAKFAST
*Tofu shake

MID-MORNING
Herb tea

LUNCH
*Tofu shake

MID-AFTERNOON
Spring water

DINNER
*Tofu shake

EVENING
Herb tea or fruit juice

DAY 2/SECOND CLEANSING DAY/SUNDAY

BREAKFAST
*Tofu shake

MID-MORNING
Grapefruit juice

LUNCH
*Tofu shake

MID-AFTERNOON
Herb tea

DINNER
*Tofu shake

EVENING
Apple juice

DAY 3/MONDAY/WEEK 1

BREAKFAST
* Tofu shake

LUNCH
Fruit

SNACK
Apple juice

DINNER
* Chicken casserole (high calcium)
Hot broccoli with lemon wedge
Hot rice
Wine
Fruit (2 servings)

SNACK
Milk (half glass)

DAY 4/TUESDAY/WEEK 1

BREAKFAST
* Tofu shake

LUNCH
Grapes (2 servings)
Roll
Milk

DINNER
* Spaghetti bolognese

Cos lettuce and cucumber with olive oil (2 teaspoons), vinegar and herbs
Bread
Wine
Fruit

SNACK
Fruit

DAY 5/WEDNESDAY/WEEK 1

BREAKFAST
* Tofu shake

LUNCH
Milk
Fruit
Wholemeal roll (½)

SNACK
Milk (half glass)

DINNER
* Codfish (grilled)
* Red cabbage
Hot new potato with
    butter
Wine
* Citrus sorbet

SNACK
Fruit

DAY 6/THURSDAY/WEEK 1

BREAKFAST
* Tofu shake
Raisin toast

LUNCH
Fruit
Roll
Milk (half glass)

DINNER
* Linguine and broccoli
    (low calorie)
Wine
Fruit

SNACK
Apple juice

DAY 7/FRIDAY/WEEK 1

BREAKFAST
★ Tofu shake

LUNCH
Fruit
Milk

DINNER
★ Caesar salad
French roll
Wine
Bananas (stewed)

DAY 8/SATURDAY/WEEK 1

BREAKFAST
★ Tofu shake

LUNCH
★ Stuffed eggs
Fruit (2 servings)
★ Poppyseed dressing
Roll

DINNER
★ Scallops with yogurt
★ Baked broccoli
★ Compote of apples
Wine

DAY 9/SUNDAY/WEEK 1

BREAKFAST
★ Tofu shake

LUNCH
Pasta salad
Apple juice

DINNER
★ Salmon bake
Hot broccoli
Wine
★ Fruit sorbet

DAY 10/MONDAY/WEEK 2

BREAKFAST
★ Tofu shake

LUNCH
Fruit
Roll
Grapefruit juice (half
  glass)

DINNER
★ Pasta shells with tomato
  sauce
Cucumber with 1 teaspoon
  olive oil, lemon juice
  and herbs
Wine

SNACK
Apple juice

DAY 11/TUESDAY/WEEK 2

BREAKFAST
★Tofu shake

LUNCH
Fruit
Roll
Apple juice

DINNER
★Chicken kebabs
Corn on the cob
Cabbage slaw with lemon
    juice, olive oil and herbs
Wine
Fruit

SNACK
Milk

DAY 12/WEDNESDAY/WEEK 2

BREAKFAST
★Tofu shake

LUNCH
Grapes
Roll
Milk (half glass)

SNACK
Apple juice

DINNER
★Vegetable caviar
Bread (2 slices)
Wine
★Citrus sorbet

SNACK
Milk (6 ounces)

DAY 13/THURSDAY/WEEK 2

BREAKFAST
★ Tofu shake

LUNCH
Fruit
Bread
Milk (half glass)

DINNER
★ Broccoli with cheese
   sauce
Cooked pasta tossed with
   olive oil
Tomato slices
Wine
★ Peach bake

SNACK
Apple juice

DAY 14/FRIDAY/WEEK 2

BREAKFAST
★ Tofu shake

SNACK
Fruit

LUNCH
Fruit
Roll
Milk

DINNER
★ Shrimp with pasta
Wine
Fruit
★ Poppyseed dressing

DAY 15/SATURDAY/WEEK 2

BREAKFAST
* Tofu shake

LUNCH
* Cream of champagne
   soup (half serving)
Hot asparagus
* Mayonnaise

DINNER
* Salmon mould
Lettuce with oil, lemon
   juice and herbs
Wine
* Citrus sorbet

DAY 16/SUNDAY/WEEK 2

BREAKFAST
* Tofu shake

SNACK
Fruit

LUNCH
Turkey breast and tomato
   sandwich
Cabbage slaw with lemon
   juice

Fruit
Milk (half glass)

DINNER
* Shrimp with dill
Cucumber
Wine
* Fruit sorbet

DAY 17/MONDAY/WEEK 3

BREAKFAST
★ Tofu shake

LUNCH
Fruit
Roll
Milk (half glass)

DINNER
★ Cheese log
Cucumber slices
Roll
Wine
Fruit

SNACK
Fruit

DAY 18/TUESDAY/WEEK 3

BREAKFAST
★ Tofu shake

LUNCH
Fruit
Roll
Apple juice

DINNER
★ Pasta with mushrooms,
    pimiento and cheese
Baby turnips
Broccoli
Lemon juice
Wine
★ Citrus sorbet

DAY 19/WEDNESDAY/WEEK 3

BREAKFAST
* Tofu shake

LUNCH
Fruit
Roll
Milk (half glass)

SNACK
Apple juice

DINNER
* Salmon (grilled)
Hot cabbage
Hot new potatoes
Parmesan cheese (1 tsp)
Wine
Fruit

SNACK
Fruit

DAY 20/THURSDAY/WEEK 3

BREAKFAST
* Tofu shake
Bread

LUNCH
Fruit
Roll
Milk

DINNER
* Vegetable-yogurt loaf
* Rice pilaf (2 servings)
Wine
Fruit (2 servings)

SNACK
Apple juice

DAY 21/FRIDAY/WEEK 3

BREAKFAST
★ Tofu shake

LUNCH
Fruit
Roll
Apple juice

DINNER
★ Lasagne
Cucumber slices
Wine

DAY 22/SATURDAY/WEEK 3

BREAKFAST
★ Tofu shake

LUNCH
Cucumber, tomato and
   pasta
★ Anchovy spread
Milk (half glass)

SNACK
Apple juice

DINNER
★ Oysters (grilled)
Lettuce and sliced radishes
   tossed with olive oil,
   lemon juice and herbs
Champagne
Fruit

SNACK
Fruit

DAY 23/SUNDAY/WEEK 3

BREAKFAST
* Tofu shake

LUNCH
* Cheesey scrambled eggs
Fruit
Milk

DINNER
* Chicken in yogurt
Cabbage slaw with lemon
  juice
Wine
Fruit

SNACK
Fruit

DAY 24/MONDAY/WEEK 4

BREAKFAST
* Tofu shake

LUNCH
Fruit
Roll
Milk (half glass)

DINNER
* Chef's salad (medium
  calcium)
Wine
Fruit
* Fruit salad dressing (2
  teaspoons)
* Citrus sorbet

SNACK
Fruit

DAY 25/TUESDAY/WEEK 4

BREAKFAST
*Tofu shake

LUNCH
Fruit
Roll
Milk (6 ounces)

DINNER
*Fettuccine with tofu
Sliced cucumber and
    tomato with olive oil,
    vinegar and herbs
Wine
*Fruit sorbet

SNACK
Apple juice

DAY 26/WEDNESDAY/WEEK 4

BREAKFAST
*Tofu shake

LUNCH
Fruit
Roll
Milk

DINNER
*Tofu croquettes
Hot baby carrots
Roll with butter
Wine
Fruit

SNACK
Apple juice

DAY 27/THURSDAY/WEEK 4

BREAKFAST
* Tofu shake

LUNCH
Fruit
Roll
Grapefruit juice

DINNER
* Salmon loaf
Pasta
Sliced cucumber
Wine
Fruit
* Fruit sorbet

SNACK
Fruit

DAY 28/FRIDAY/WEEK 4

BREAKFAST
* Tofu shake
Raisin bread

LUNCH
Fruit
Roll
Milk (half glass)

SNACK
Fruit

DINNER
* Omelette with tofu and
   cheese
Lettuce and cauliflower
   with lemon juice
Wine
Fruit
* Poppyseed dressing

SNACK
Fruit

DAY 29/SATURDAY/WEEK 4

BREAKFAST
★ Tofu shake

LUNCH
★ Shrimp dip
Cauliflower florets
Cucumber spears
Milk

DINNER
Chicken breast grilled with
  lemon juice and herbs
Pasta
Hot cabbage with herbs
  and lemon juice
Wine
★ Cherry sauce with sorbet
  ($\frac{1}{2}$ serving)

SNACK
Fruit

DAY 30/SUNDAY/WEEK 4

BREAKFAST
★ Tofu shake

LUNCH
★ Sea salad
Milk (half glass)
Fruit

DINNER
★ Ravioli
Fruit
Wine

A High-calcium, Lactose-free, Low-calorie Diet

Some people are unable to digest lactose, making it impossible for them to consume milk and other dairy products. None the less, such people can still have a diet rich in calcium and other nutrients while losing weight. This is possible because some vegetables, fish and shellfish have two, three or even four times as much calcium as calories. Some of these foods are broccoli, cabbage, onions, artichokes, sardines and anchovies. Oranges, oysters, cauliflower and cucumber all have high calcium-to-calorie ratios as well.

The following week-long, high-calcium, low-calorie diet is without lactose. Be sure that in addition you drink four pints (2.4 litres) of water each day.

MONDAY

BREAKFAST
Orange sections (2
    servings)
Roll

LUNCH
Fruit
Roll

DINNER
Canned salmon (2
    servings)
Pasta shells (2 servings)
Broccoli and butterhead
    lettuce
Wine

TUESDAY

BREAKFAST
Orange sections
Rolls

LUNCH
Fruit
* Poppyseed dressing
* Stuffed eggs (2 servings)

DINNER
Shrimp steamed with dill
    and lemon
Asparagus
Raw broccoli with lemon
    juice (2 servings)
Wine
Fruit

WEDNESDAY

BREAKFAST
Orange sections (2
   servings)
Roll

LUNCH
Lettuce
Tomato
Cucumber and onions
Oil and vinegar
Fruit

DINNER
Sardines in tomato sauce
Rice
Broccoli
Wine
Fruit

THURSDAY

BREAKFAST
Orange sections (2
   servings)
Rolls (2)

LUNCH
Hard-boiled egg
Lettuce
Tofu cubes
Apple sauce
Tomato
Onion

Lemon juice
Fruit

DINNER
Hot pasta tossed with
   anchovies, tomato,
   broccoli (2 servings) and
   lemon juice
Wine
Fruit

FRIDAY

BREAKFAST
Orange sections (2
  servings)
Rolls (2)

LUNCH
Raw broccoli (2 servings)
Bread (1 slice)
Cucumber

DINNER
Grilled salmon (7 ounces)
Hot kale
Wine
Fruit

SATURDAY

BREAKFAST
Orange sections (2
  servings)
Rolls (2)

LUNCH
Cabbage slaw (2 servings)
  with lemon juice
Tofu cubes
Pineapple
White grapes (2 servings)

DINNER
Shrimp, steamed
Baby peas
Raw broccoli (2 servings)
and cauliflower with
  mayonnaise
Wine

SUNDAY

BREAKFAST
Orange sections (2 servings)
Rolls (2)

LUNCH
Raw broccoli (2 servings)
Cucumber with lemon juice
Wholemeal roll
Apple

DINNER
Oysters (2 servings) with hot sauce
Chilled pasta with chicory, onion and lemon juice
Wine
Fruit

CHAPTER TEN

SUPPLEMENTS

The most frequent question that we are asked after we have given a talk about the benefits of vitamin D and calcium is: What do you recommend as a supplement? We usually answer this with a few questions to the person who asked us, such as whether the person is intolerant of milk.

There are no long-term studies of the effect of supplements on the risk of almost any disease. But there are a number of studies on the effect of food. It is clear that food containing vitamin D and calcium reduces risk of certain cancers and other calcium-deficiency related diseases. We use a conservative approach, and recommend that people obtain calcium and vitamin D from natural foods in their diet together with a small amount contained in a daily vitamin and mineral tablet.

It has been estimated that within the UK, just under 5 per cent of the white European population and up to 75 per cent of the non-white population have difficulty digesting the natural sugar in milk called lactose. If you can't tolerate lactose, you will have to try alternatives to milk. Some people who can't tolerate milk seem to be able to tolerate yogurt. Yogurt is a rich source of calcium (200–225 milligrams per 125 gram pot) and will supply the calcium you need. Look for brands that contain only milk and active *Bacillus acidophilis, Bacillus bulgaris* or similar cultures. Avoid brands that contain carrageenan, a chemical that produces an intestinal disease, ulcerative colitis, in animals. Although carrageenan is a permitted food additive we feel its use in foods should be discontinued pending appropriate epidemiological studies. Eat low-fat yogurt whenever possible.

If you cannot eat yogurt, or simply do not like yogurt, there are other possibilities. Lactose can be removed from milk with lactase enzymes. Milk is now available with much of the lactose removed and you may be able to tolerate it better. If you are trying yogurt or lactose-reduced milk for the first time, begin with a small amount – say a tablespoon or two – working up to larger amounts only if you can tolerate the small ones.

If you try these options, and others, such as fish, tofu and vegetables containing high usable calcium, as shown in the calcium counter at the back of the book, and still can't get your calcium level to the 800 to 1,200 milligrams recommended per day, you may need a calcium supplement.

There are several criteria you should use in picking a supplement: *Absorption*, or the amount of calcium absorbed per milligram of calcium present in the tablet; *Tolerance*, or how well your body accepts the supplement; *Side effects* (see Chapter 12); *Special situations*, such as existing diseases for which supplements could create problems; *Interactions*, or problems that could occur because you are taking another medicine at the same time as the supplement; and *Cost*, since you don't want to pay more than is necessary for safe, effective supplementation.

Calcium supplements should be taken only after individual evaluation and advice of a doctor or dietician, particularly in children or anyone who is bedridden. Children can usually get enough calcium from food alone and do not require calcium supplements, except on the advice of a paediatrician. People who are bedridden usually do not need supplements, since inactivity causes calcium levels in the blood to rise as bone mass drops. Adding calcium can create trouble in such people.

Unfortunately, manufacturers of calcium carbonate tablets and other calcium preparations have yet to show that calcium works as well in the form of tablets as it does in food. Several years ago (1982), an epidemiological study by our colleague Dr Richard Shekelle and his colleagues in Chicago showed a benefit of vitamin A in preventing cancer of the lung in smokers. Smokers purchased vitamin A pills in hope of achieving a similar effect. What they did not know was that the form of vitamin A that had produced the benefit, carotene, was very different from the retinol form that was then being sold over the counter in most states. Carotene is a pigment common in nature and has powerful anti-oxidant properties that prevent various reactions within the body. Retinol is a much poorer anti-oxidant. The vitamin people took in the form of supplements probably did them little good, as it was probably the anti-oxidant properties more than the other characteristics of carotene that provided the protection.

Vitamin D

The number of foods containing vitamin D is limited. We feel it would be beneficial if the dairy industry added small amounts of vitamin D to milk, yogurt, cottage cheese and other dairy products in order to provide a range of choices for the consumer.

Perhaps the most common complaint about consumption of foods containing vitamin D is that many of them are high in calories. But by making careful choices, calories can be kept low. Fish, for example, provides vitamin D, as well as the omega-3 fatty acids that protect against heart disease.

Skimmed milk contains large amounts of calcium *and* vitamin D, and there are only 77 calories in an eight-ounce glass (as well as 304 milligrams of calcium).

Use vitamins in moderation. Too many people have a

tendency to think they are well nourished if they swallow the latest multivitamin pill and skip foods that might provide such vitamins naturally. Many of the secrets of preventing cancer and other diseases are not yet available in a vitamin bottle. It's true that we live in a pill-oriented age. But the more we resist the notion that a vitamin or other kind of pill will take care of all our needs, the better off we are likely to be. You would accomplish more by choosing a salmon steak for dinner, drinking skimmed milk, eating yogurt and fresh fruit, taking the time to prepare fresh vegetables, exercising and using *The Calcium Diet*.

Calcium Carbonate

At the moment calcium carbonate seems to be the best of the calcium supplements. It provides the largest dose per tablet of calcium of anything available. It doesn't seem to differ much from other calcium supplements in absorbability in healthy adults.

If you drop a calcium carbonate tablet in a glass of water, it will not dissolve. Calcium carbonate is relatively insoluble in ordinary water. Most drinking water, of course, already contains calcium – it is the principal ingredient that makes water hard (it's the white powder left behind in the coffee pot or the saucepan when you boil hard water). If you add some lemon juice or vinegar to the water, however, the calcium carbonate will dissolve. Normally, this is the job your stomach accomplishes when you eat a meal rich in calcium. Eating causes your stomach to release hydrochloric acid, and in an acid medium, the tablet dissolves.

This makes calcium carbonate a good choice if you decide to use supplements and you are healthy. But some people don't have enough hydrochloric acid on tap in their stomach. This deficiency is known as achlorhydria and is common in the elderly. If you lack enough acid, swallowing a calcium carbonate tablet will be almost like dropping it in a glass of plain water. It will not dissolve in your stomach. There is a chance that some of it will dissolve elsewhere in your gastrointestinal system, because bacteria can sometimes produce acids that will help aid calcium digestion. But the benefits of taking calcium carbonate will be substantially reduced.

There is another potential drawback to using calcium carbonate supplements. In places throughout the world where sanitation is poor, acid in the stomach provides a barrier against harmful organisms present in food and water. A lot of common organisms that cause disease are killed by acids when they enter the stomach. The acid therefore serves a dual role: it helps digest food and also reduces the bacterial count and helps to prevent disease. Calcium carbonate tends to *reduce* the acidity of the stomach. When the stomach is neutralized by regular intake of calcium supplements, the acid barrier against bacteria may be weakened. Food and water sanitation is generally excellent in the U K, so the problem here is minimal. But if you travel extensively or live somewhere where food and water sanitation is marginal, you may want to restrict or reduce your calcium carbonate intake.

Calcium carbonate is both the cheapest and the most readily available kind of calcium supplement. It can be found in chemists and health-food shops in certain over-the-counter products. Check labels carefully.

If you do decide to take calcium carbonate supplements, be careful not to consume them with calcium robbers, as much of the calcium would be bound up and made unusable.

Calcium Gluconate

This compound is similar to that of calcium carbonate. Calcium gluconate is made by combining calcium with glucose, the simplest sugar. Calcium gluconate is probably tolerated by most people as well as calcium carbonate.

Calcium gluconate contains only 9 per cent elemental calcium. If you choose this supplement, you will need to take a great many more tablets to get a reasonable amount of calcium. Like calcium carbonate, this supplement is best taken with meals, because calcium in general dissolves better in acid. Calcium gluconate is somewhat more expensive than calcium carbonate, which may affect your choice of supplement.

Calcium Lactate

This preparation contains about 13 per cent calcium. With calcium lactate, you don't need to worry about neutralization of stomach acid as much as with calcium carbonate. As with other forms of calcium supplements, calcium lactate is best taken with meals. Again, be careful not to include calcium robbers with your meal, in order to obtain the full benefit from the calcium supplement.

Other Preparations

There are several preparations of calcium that we do not recommend. Bone meal is one. It is made from ground animal bones. Animals are subject to the same pollution that we are and many absorb lead and other pollutants, storing them in their bones. When you consume bone meal you are consuming an animal's lifetime of stored pollutants – not much of a bargain. Oyster shells, too, are pulverized and sold as calcium supplements. Their safety and purity depends upon where the oysters were harvested. If they were from an area contaminated with industrial waste, such as lead, the oyster shells can incorporate the lead and pass it on to you. Dolomite, an ancient chalky compound, may also contain contaminants such as lead and arsenic. We recommend that you avoid these sources of calcium supplementation. It is especially important to avoid them for infants, children and women who are pregnant or nursing.

Other calcium compounds are sometimes recommended as supplements but none have the safety of calcium carbonate, calcium lactate and calcium gluconate.

When calcium is consumed in food, it is usually in beverages or foods that are high in water content. Milk is mostly water, and many vegetables have high water content along with calcium. Water ensures that the calcium will be soluble in the stomach and in the intestine so that it can be absorbed. It also prevents the formation of crystals of calcium oxalate, calcium phosphate and other compounds in the kidneys that can lead to kidney stones. One of the reasons that food is safer than supplements is because of water content. If you must supplement your diet with calcium tablets, be sure to drink at least four pints (2.4 litres) of water per day.

Several grocery shop items contain added calcium such as orange or grapefruit drinks. The producers of these products mean well, but because they are not natural foods – only part fruit juice – the added calcium is not necessarily a good trade-off. None the less, in terms of calcium these drinks are safer than supplements, because of the fluid content. In addition, some soft drinks also have added calcium, but the amount is not enough to be beneficial.

CHAPTER ELEVEN

THE IMPORTANCE OF WATER

The fact is, we can't live without water. Two thirds of the water we consume goes directly into our cells. The rest goes into the bloodstream and the spaces surrounding the cells. All tissues in the body allow water to pass through. No other liquid has this distinction.

Your body is finely tuned to retain a constant concentration of body fluids. It does this very precisely by retaining water in proportion to anything dissolved in the body fluids. When we need to dilute salt or sugar, for example, because the concentration has risen, cells in a part of our brain called the hypothalamus send out a signal. We interpret the signal as thirst. When we dilute the salt and sugar enough, we are no longer thirsty.

It is important with the Calcium Diet that you drink plenty of water and liquids throughout the day. Water is essential to a healthy body, and will help you to dissolve and absorb the increased calcium that you take in, whether from food or from supplements.

Although you may not realize it, the dietary substance with the highest calcium-to-calorie ratio is water. Some water contains as much as 100 milligrams of calcium per litre and has no calories. Unless you live in a city where the calcium levels are high, you'll have to get most of your daily calcium from the food you eat. If you do live in a city where the calcium level per litre of water approaches 100 milligrams, however, you may be able, by drinking two litres a day, to obtain one sixth of our recommended daily calcium intake from water alone.

If you're worried about taking in too much calcium

because your city water supply is high in calcium, rest assured that there is no danger. According to the American National Academy of Sciences, there has never been a report of acute toxicity from consumption of the calcium contained in ordinary amounts of food or drinking water. Drink as much water as you like. In fact, it is unwise to take in large amounts of calcium *without* also taking in lots of fluids, because calcium can't be absorbed well or excreted safely without water. Fluids are excellent vehicles for calcium.

Drinking water with high levels of calcium can also help in other ways. A high intake of calcium decreases absorption of lead and other toxic trace metals from the intestine. It has been shown that the amount of calcium in the blood is inversely related to the amount of lead.

Calcium also prevents intestinal absorption of cadmium, a trace metal that can cause serious diseases. Cadmium can make the body produce lower than usual levels of vitamin D, which is important for active absorption of calcium. This creates a vicious cycle leading to still less absorption of calcium and eventually to bone damage.

According to the American National Academy of Sciences, 'No upper limit for calcium in drinking water needs to be set to protect public health. In cases of calcium deficiencies, the presence of this element in drinking water provides nutritional benefit.'

Bottled Water

Almost all bottled waters are bacteriologically pure. Because of that, purity is not a significant factor in choosing a bottled water. In that sense, it doesn't matter *where* a water is from, since there is no reason to believe that water from one state or country, such as Arkansas or France, is any different structurally from water anywhere else. What does differ is the chemical content of the water.

There are three types of bottled water used for drinking. The first is distilled or deionized water, which is water from which all the elements have been removed by boiling or putting it through a device known as a deionizer. It is not wise to consume distilled or deionized water on a daily basis because it contains no trace calcium or other minerals.

The second kind of water used for drinking is spring water, or 'drinking water'. Spring water comes out of the earth on its own pressure without piping, although a short pipe is permitted in the spring. If the water doesn't come out of the ground on its own, it is not spring water. Such water is usually called well water, although it is sometimes called 'mountain' or 'natural' water. The term 'drinking water' is also widely used, but has no meaning. It can apply to anything from deionized or distilled water, spring or well water, to municipal water that may have been deionized.

Finally there is mineral water, which may contain large amounts of sodium, since sodium content is not subject to meaningful restrictions. People with high blood pressure should avoid mineral water unless they know it is low in sodium.

Because the calcium content in bottled water is rarely provided on the label, it is usually impossible to know how much calcium you may be getting from bottled water if you consume it on a daily basis.

The Differences in Municipal Water

Water varies drastically from region to region, and even between different areas of a city. There may be more than one source of water supplying a city and many different sources supplying a geographical region of Britain. For example, Sheffield in south Yorkshire shows a variation in total hardness of water (calcium and magnesium – expressed as milligrams of calcium carbonate in a litre of water) of 70 to 150 milligrams per litre. The north-east of Britain varies in total hardness from 50 milligrams in Durham to 350 milligrams in Hartlepool. (See Appendix B: Drinking Water in Major UK Cities.)

If your regional water supply is low in calcium, you'll have to make special efforts to be sure to get enough calcium from your diet. Unfortunately, most bottled waters, whether mineral or spring water, do not list the calcium content in them. So if you drink bottled water primarily, you'll have no way of knowing how much calcium you're getting from the water. To ensure that you get enough calcium daily, assume that the spring water you drink has no calcium, and gauge your daily calcium intake from the foods you eat.

Hard Water

Hard water refers to water with high concentrations of calcium and magnesium. We have now learned that hard water can have health benefits. According to a report from the American National Academy of Sciences in 1979, studies of large geographic areas have found that hard water is linked with low rates of heart disease. The scientific panel reported that drinking soft water might increase risk of heart disease by as much as 25 per cent, and risk of stroke and hypertension by as much as 20 per cent.

The epidemiological evidence strongly suggests that soft water is not as healthy as hard water. We are surprised when we hear that a public water supply system is softening its water, because the methods used for water softening cut water's calcium content and usually raise the sodium content. The likely result: a slightly increased risk of hypertension, heart disease and stroke in people who drink the water.

Home water softeners are just as bad in terms of health. Most home water softeners remove one atom of calcium or magnesium and replace it with two atoms of sodium. It's an unwise practice.

The Danger of Aluminium

One of the chemicals found in the water you drink is aluminium. High doses of aluminium can interfere with absorption of calcium. Until 1974 aluminium was regarded as a non-toxic material. Recent studies have changed that viewpoint. Aluminium is found in unusually high concentrations in the tissues of the nervous system of people who have Alzheimer's disease. We don't know whether this is due to build-up of aluminium from water or foods, but it is a finding that has stirred considerable interest.

Why is aluminium so dangerous? Like calcium, aluminium is a positively charged ion – a cation. Like calcium it is a metal. When tissues in your body need calcium, they send out an SOS informing the body. When the need can't be met by calcium, the hungry cells absorb aluminium instead.

People on kidney dialysis absorb aluminium from water entering dialysis machines and sometimes develop aluminium poisoning. This causes a type of dementia very similar to Alzheimer's disease, and is the leading cause of death in long-term dialysis patients.

CHAPTER TWELVE

SIDE EFFECTS

No discussion of a programme to increase dietary calcium is complete without consideration of possible side effects and how you can minimize them. Fortunately, the side effects of calcium are almost nonexistent at levels found in the normal diet. But the side effects of large overdoses of vitamin D can be serious.

The Department of Health estimates that adults in the UK consume an average of 800–1,000 milligrams of calcium per day. We take in about 10 per cent less if we live in cities, about 10 per cent more if we live in farming areas. Some people consume 2,000 milligrams of calcium per day with no apparent toxicity or side effects.

People who treat their own indigestion or ulcers by taking large amounts of antacids, some of which are high in calcium compounds, may develop *milk-alkali syndrome*, which deposits calcium in unusual places in the body. This is uncommon, however, and is usually readily reversed by cutting down on antacids. But the risk of developing the syndrome is virtually nonexistent for those who obtain calcium from ordinary foods and beverages. It is, however, one reason we do not recommend calcium supplements. If you are taking antacids on your own advice, or on the advice of your doctor, consult your doctor before adding further calcium to your diet.

The daily intakes of calcium shown in the table on page 85 should not be exceeded. These recommendations are in general similar to those of the American National Academy of Sciences, with corrections for people living in areas of low ultraviolet light.

Your body very carefully regulates its absorption of calcium. If you take in too much, the intestine will absorb less. On the average, only about 15 to 35 per cent of the calcium we consume is absorbed (partly because much of the calcium we consume is bound in chemical compounds which make it unusable). If your body is deficient in calcium, the intestine tries to compensate, absorbing more.

Vitamin D

It is impossible to get an overdose of vitamin D from exposure to the sun, although with excessive exposure you *can* cause sunburn, and raise your risk of skin cancer. It is also almost impossible to get an overdose of vitamin D from milk or other sources in the diet.

It is, however, possible to get too much vitamin D from vitamin supplements. People have been known to take in 50,000 IU or more of vitamin D per day. While large doses such as this can sometimes be administered safely under the close supervision of a doctor for treatment of specific medical problems, taken by a healthy person, such large doses can increase the body's demand for calcium beyond what an ordinary diet can provide. The result depends upon the degree of overdose. An excessive amount of vitamin D can lead to hypercalcification or excessive deposition of calcium throughout the body, including the kidneys, as well as excessive loss of calcium from bone, the opposite effect of what is produced by ordinary dietary vitamin D sources.

The daily intake of vitamin D is difficult to assess because of the variation in the amount of vitamin D that people gain from sunlight. However, to safeguard against inadequate intakes, particularly during the winter, it is recommended in the UK that infants receive 300 IU of vitamin D per day and children and adults 400 I U. *The dose for children should never be exceeded.* For most adults, there is a larger margin of safety, and the restriction on intake need not be as rigid. Adults aged eighteen years and over can take in vitamin D from ordinary foods in any reasonable amount with minimal risk. But we do not advise that any healthy person supplements his or her diet with vitamin D in pill or other concentrated forms, except for the amount found in a single ordinary multiple vitamin tablet per day. We strongly caution against the use of any vitamin D supplement in infants or in pregnant or lactating women. If such a supplement is used, it is very important that the daily dose from all sources does not exceed 400 I U in infants and 600 I U in pregnant or lactating women.

Occasionally some individuals are hypersensitive to vitamin D and subject to some toxicity, even at lower dosages. These effects appear to be reversible. Severe cases of infantile hypercalcemia have occurred due to excessive vitamin D supplementation, including some cases possibly induced in utero by excessive supplementary vitamin D taken by the mother. Such excessive supplementation of vitamin D from pills and capsules can induce a syndrome in infants that includes low birth weight and mental, cardiovascular and renal complications. For this reason we do not recommend any form of supplementation of vitamin D except for that in ordinary foods, and a daily vitamin and mineral supplement (see page 86). We particularly recommend that children and pregnant women do not receive vitamin D supplementation other than in foods, and only in special cases.

Kidney Stones

The cause of kidney stones is still largely unknown. People with infections, various diseases, certain genetic defects and dehydration are at particular risk. Most kidney stones contain at least some calcium, but dietary intake of calcium has not been shown conclusively to play a role in causing them. As a precaution, doctors usually limit patients with a history of kidney stones (and in some cases patients with a family history of them) to no more than 400 milligrams per day of calcium. This limitation is the subject of considerable controversy since calcium deficiency may result. Patients are also prohibited from drinking vitamin-D-fortified milk or eating other foods rich in vitamin D.

Approximately seventy-five per cent of kidney stones in patients in the United Kingdom also contain oxalates. There is no standard diet for the reduction of oxalates, but tables are available showing the amount of oxalates in foods (see Appendix E). Most experts on kidney stones believe that it is not calcium intake that causes kidney stones, but rather excess oxalates in the urine that combines with calcium to create the stone.

Excess oxalates in some people may be simply a result of their metabolism. Because of their genetic make-up, they produce more oxalates in the urine, increasing their risk of kidney stones. At this point, it may be impossible to do much about genetically caused excess. But other people have high levels of oxalates in urine because they consume too many foods that are rich in oxalates. Intake of dietary oxalates for people who have formed stones, or who have a family history of them, should not exceed 40 to 50 milligrams per day.

A surprisingly varied number of foods contain high concentrations of oxalates. Swiss chard, spinach, rhubarb and even tea are examples. Further information on oxalates in the diet is available in a book by D. M. Ney and associates, entitled *The Low Oxalate Diet Book for the Prevention of Oxalate Kidney Stones*, published by the

University of California, San Diego. If you have had kidney stones or have a family history of them, consult your doctor before making any changes in your diet with regard to either oxalates or calcium.

Rare Diseases

There are a few rare diseases for which calcium intake should be restricted. One example is a skin disease called pseudoxanthoma elasticum. Some scientists have suggested that lowering dietary calcium in people with this rare disease might minimize its clinical effects. If you have this disease, your calcium intake should be carefully monitored with the advice of your doctor. Another such disease is sarcoidosis, a relatively uncommon disease that affects various body organs and which can result in overly high levels of calcium in the blood. Another disease where calcium intake must be closely monitored is primary hypercalciuria, which is excessive urinary excretion of calcium. People who have this disease should consult their doctor before altering their calcium or vitamin D intake.

We also advise any patients who are on kidney dialysis to consult with their doctor about their calcium intake, since dialysis interferes with ordinary metabolism of calcium.

We have located one report of a two-year-old girl with pure calcium carbonate gallstones, possibly related to the calcium carbonate supplement her mother took during the last four months of pregnancy. The scientists who reported this stated that they knew of no other such reports. Pregnant women who take calcium supplements should discuss their intake with their obstetricians.

A study of Craig L. Stemmar and associates at the University of Miami Medical School in Florida showed that use of antacids containing magnesium hydroxide and aluminium hydroxide results in a tenfold increase in alkalinity of urine. Because calcium may form stones more readily in alkaline urine, large intakes of such antacids are unwise.

Other Side Effects

Calcium carbonate tends to reduce the acidity of the stomach. Many people take calcium carbonate as an antacid. Millions of people seem to be able to take calcium carbonate tablets without complications. But such users have probably had excessive acid in the stomach that may have splashed into the oesophagus. The tablets may have briefly neutralized some of the acid. For people who do *not* have excessive stomach acid, routine consumption of calcium carbonate could overly neutralize stomach contents. The effects of such neutralization are not known.

One last cautionary note concerns medication for ulcers. Cimetidine is one of the most widely prescribed drugs in the UK. It helps cure ulcers by interfering with gastric secretion. If you are on this or other drugs that produce similar effects, you may not have enough acid in your stomach to dissolve calcium carbonate tablets, particularly if you take them between meals. For such people we recommend increasing calcium intake only through dietary calcium in foods and milk.

CHAPTER THIRTEEN

A FINAL NOTE

You are the key to the success of this book. The Calcium Diet programme will help you to achieve a longer, healthier life – but only if you follow the guidelines the programme provides for increasing your calcium intake safely. There is no magic involved. If your diet has been calcium-deficient for twenty years, and you begin to suffer the effects of osteoporosis, increasing your dietary calcium will not suddenly reverse the osteoporosis that has taken so many years to develop. The same is true for cancer. To benefit from the Calcium Diet programme and diet, you must begin *now*.

It is a discipline that should last for the rest of your life. But it is not a difficult programme to follow. All that we ask is that you eat fresh, good-tasting food – foods that are high in natural calcium – and avoid those few foods that would deplete your calcium supply. The rewards are many.

Establishing a new routine is a challenge. How great the challenge is, and how well you will be able to cope with it, depends on how strongly you're motivated. Decide now that you are going to make a habit of the schedule outlined in this book. Once you've followed it for a month or two, you'll find that being careful to eat enough calcium-rich foods will become second nature. After all, a longer, healthier life is certainly worth the effort.

Proper dietary levels of calcium and vitamin D will cut your risk of death from breast and intestinal cancers, and, by following the programme now, cut your risk of osteoporosis.

A proper dietary intake of calcium will also bring your blood pressure down a few points. As your blood pressure drops, your risk of heart disease – the number one cause of death in the UK – will be lowered. The diet's low level of saturated fat will also cut your risk of heart disease and you'll decrease your risk of stroke, another prime cause of death in older adults. The risk will be cut even more by the high level of potassium from fresh fruits and vegetables in the diet, which also helps reduce the risk of stroke.

It is a fact that in countries where people consume large amounts of vitamin D and calcium the average life span tends to be longer. The Japanese, for example, have the highest level of dietary vitamin D in the world; they also have the longest life spans. Life expectancy in Japanese men is seventy-three years, and seventy-eight years in women. High levels of consumption of vitamin D from foods alone are consistent with a long life span.

Begin your road to health and longevity by starting the Calcium Diet now.

PART THREE

THE CALCIUM DIET RECIPES

The following are the recipes for the starred dishes listed in the calcium diet in Chapter 8 and the calcium-rich weight-loss diet in Chapter 9. We have also included some additional recipes for variety. Each recipe yields four servings.

ANCHOVY SPREAD

   375 g/13.5 oz plain low-fat yogurt
   1 tablespoon spring onions, chopped fine
   1 teaspoon paprika
   2-ounce can anchovy fillets
   ½ teaspoon caraway seed
   Pepper
   1 teaspoon capers

Beat together (or process in a food processor) all ingredients except capers. Stir in capers. Pack into a crock or bowl, and refrigerate for 2 to 4 hours to blend flavours. Serve on french bread or mix with pasta and vegetables.

Note: For a higher-calcium variation, see Anchovy Spread below.

ANCHOVY SPREAD (HIGH CALCIUM)

375 g/13.5 oz plain low-fat yogurt
1 tablespoon spring onions, chopped fine
1 teaspoon paprika
2-oz can anchovy fillets
½ teaspoon caraway seed
Pepper
285 g/10 oz tofu
1 teaspoon capers

Beat together (or process in a food processor) all ingredients except capers. Stir in capers. Pack into a crock or bowl, and refrigerate for 2 to 4 hours to blend flavours. Serve on french bread or mix with pasta and vegetables.

APPLE-CRANBERRY MOULD

1 envelope unflavoured gelatine
375 ml/13.5 fl. oz plus 2 teaspoons cold water
120 g/4 oz fructose
340 g/12 oz fresh cranberries
180 g/6 oz apples, skinned and diced

Soften the gelatine in 2 teaspoons of cold water. In a large saucepan, combine 375 ml water with the fructose and bring to a boil. Add cranberries and simmer for 20 minutes. Remove from heat and stir in the gelatine until dissolved. Cool the mixture and add apples. Pour into 1½-quart mould, then chill. Remove from the mould and serve on a cold plate.

APPLE CRUMBLE

4 medium cooking apples
1 teaspoon cinnamon
125 ml/4 fl oz water
100 g/3.5 oz fructose
60 g/2 oz enriched flour
60 g/2 oz safflower margarine

Preheat oven to 375°F/190°C/Gas 5. Peel and core the apples, and cut them crosswise in ½-inch-thick slices. Arrange the slices in a nonstick casserole, and sprinkle with cinnamon. Add the water.

Rub together the fructose, flour and margarine, creating a crumbly mixture. Sprinkle this over the apples. Bake uncovered for 45 minutes. Serve warm.

Optional: Top with small scoops of sorbet.

BAKED APPLES

4 large apples
250 ml/½ pt water
½ lemon, peeled
1 tablespoon raisins
100 g/3.5 oz fructose
90 g/3 oz clover honey
1 teaspoon cinnamon
250 ml/½ pt water

Core (but do not peel) the apples, taking care not to pierce the bottoms. Remove the top quarter of each apple. Place the apples in a baking dish. Add the water to the dish.

Cut the lemon into small fragments of pulp, and combine with the raisins and half the fructose. Spoon this mixture into the apple cavities.

Preheat the oven to 350°F/180°C/Gas 4. Mix the honey, water, cinnamon and remaining fructose in a saucepan and boil for 4 minutes. Spoon this mixture over the apples. Bake until tender, for about one hour.

BANANAS (STEWED)

   4 tablespoons safflower margarine
   4 tablespoons fructose
   3 firm bananas
   4 tablespoons sherry
   150 ml/6 oz orange juice

Melt the margarine in a saucepan. Add fructose. Then add bananas sliced lengthwise, cooking until slightly browned. Pour in the sherry and orange juice. Simmer for 10 minutes in liquid. Serve hot, pouring the sauce over the fruit.

BLACKBERRY PUDDING

   2 pints of blackberries
   250 ml/½ pt water
   6 pieces of day-old white bread, crusts removed
   6 tablespoons blackberry wine

Stew the blackberries in water by bringing to a boil and simmering 3 to 4 minutes. Let cool.

Break the bread into chunks and line the bottom of a ceramic casserole with them. Cover the bread with part of the stewed blackberries. Continue making alternate layers until dish is filled. Chill in refrigerator overnight. Serve with blackberry wine spooned over the top.

BLUEBERRY BUNS

300 ml/½ pt skimmed milk
60 g/2 oz sugar
60 g/2 oz honey
60 ml/ 2 oz safflower oil
2 packets yeast
60 ml/2 oz water, lukewarm
400 g/14 oz flour
340 g/12 oz fresh blueberries
60 ml/2 oz melted butter

Scald the milk and combine with honey and safflower oil. Cool until lukewarm. Soften yeast in a large bowl of water. Add the lukewarm milk mixture and stir in enough flour to make the dough stiff. Turn the dough onto a lightly floured surface and knead until smooth. Set dough in a greased bowl and brush oil over surface. Cover with a towel and put in a warm place until dough doubles in size (about one hour). Spread the dough out on unfloured surface. Divide in half and roll each half into a rectangle, about ¼-inch thick and 10 inches long. Brush with milk.

Mix the sugar and blueberries together gently. Sprinkle half the mixture on each half of dough. Roll up each section gently as if to make a swiss roll. Cut the rolls into ten equal portions. Place on greased baking pans. Brush with melted butter. Cover with greaseproof paper and leave to rise for one hour.

Preheat oven to 350°F/180°C/Gas 4. Bake 30 minutes. Serve with tofu whipped cream for a special touch.

BAKED BROCCOLI

> 3 spears of broccoli, medium-sized (approximately 1 pound)
> Safflower margarine
> Dash of pepper
> Juice of 1 lemon
> 2 tablespoons olive oil
> 3 tablespoons parmesan cheese

Preheat oven to 350°F/180°C/Gas 4. Cut broccoli spears into florets. Lay in casserole dish greased with safflower margarine. Mix all other ingredients and spread over top. Bake for 30 minutes.

Note: For a higher-calcium variation, see Baked Broccoli below.

BAKED BROCCOLI (HIGH CALCIUM)

> 6 medium-sized spears of broccoli (approximately 2 pounds)
> Safflower margarine
> Dash of pepper
> Juice of 1 lemon
> 4 tablespoons corn oil
> 1 tablespoon dijon mustard
> 6 tablespoons parmesan cheese

Preheat oven to 350°F/180°C/Gas 4. Cut broccoli spears into florets. Lay in casserole dish greased with safflower margarine. Mix all other ingredients and spread over top. Bake for 30 minutes.

BROCCOLI SOUP

450 g/1 lb broccoli
2 cloves garlic, minced
1.5 l/2.75 pts water
1 fresh tomato, cubed
120 g/4 oz spaghetti, broken into 2-inch pieces
Pepper
2 tablespoons olive oil
6 tablespoons grated parmesan cheese

Wash and drain broccoli. Soak for 20 minutes in cool water. Cut into inch-size florets. Put in pan with garlic, water and tomato. Bring to a boil over a high flame, then simmer for 10 minutes. Add pasta and sprinkle with pepper. Cook for 15 more minutes, stirring occasionally, or until 'al dente'. Spoon olive oil over top. Cook 3 minutes longer. Sprinkle grated parmesan cheese on top.

BROCCOLI WITH CHEESE SAUCE

150 g/5 oz tofu
2 tablespoons virgin olive oil
4 tablespoons parmesan cheese
1 teaspoon dry mustard
1 teaspoon lemon juice
1 clove of garlic, pressed
450 g/1 lb broccoli

Stir tofu, oil, cheese, mustard, lemon juice and garlic together. Place in a double boiler and blend with a whisk while warming. Trim the broccoli florets from the stems and steam until tender. Drain and serve immediately topped with the warm sauce.

CAESAR SALAD

1 clove garlic
60 ml/2 oz olive oil
2 heads firm, crisp lettuce
1 head soft lettuce
Pepper
1 egg
Juice of 2 lemons
16–20 drops worcestershire sauce
1 tablespoon parmesan cheese, grated
50 g/2 oz croutons

Dice garlic and place in oil for several hours.

Tear lettuces into a salad bowl. Pour the garlic olive oil mixture over it. Sprinkle fresh ground pepper on top and toss gently once or twice.

Coddle the egg (boil for 1 minute). Break the egg into a bowl and whip lightly with lemon juice and worcestershire sauce. Add to salad while tossing 2 to 3 times. Sprinkle cheese and croutons over top and toss lightly

Note: For a higher-calcium variation, see Caesar Salad below.

CAESAR SALAD (HIGH CALCIUM)

1 clove garlic
60 ml/2 oz olive oil
2 heads crisp lettuce
1 head soft lettuce
Pepper
100 g/3.5 oz parmesan cheese, grated
1 egg

Juice of 2 lemons
16–20 drops worcestershire sauce
50 g/2 oz croutons
3 anchovies (optional)

Dice garlic and place in oil for several hours.

Tear lettuces into salad bowl. Pour the garlic olive oil mixture over it. Sprinkle fresh ground pepper on top and toss gently once or twice.

Coddle the egg (boil for 1 minute). Break the egg into a bowl and whip lightly with lemon juice and worcestershire sauce. Add to salad while tossing 2 to 3 times. Sprinkle cheese and croutons over top and toss lightly. Top with thin strips of anchovy.

CAULIFLOWER WITH CRAB

1 medium head cauliflower
1 can crab bisque
125 g/4.5 oz yogurt
1 tablespoon dry mustard
Dash of pepper

Break cauliflower into florets. Steam for 10 minutes or microwave for 2 to 3 minutes. Heat the soup until hot, but not boiling, then stir in the yogurt. Add dry mustard and pepper. Stir mixture over cauliflower.

CHEESE LOG

450 g/1 lb low-fat cottage cheese
120 g/4 oz blue cheese

120 g/4 oz cheddar cheese spread
1 teaspoon worcestershire sauce
¼ teaspoon onion juice
Pinch of paprika
2 cucumbers

Mix the three cheeses, worcestershire sauce, and onion juice together. On wax paper shape the mixture into a long roll or ball. Roll in paprika. Chill overnight. Serve on cucumber slices.

CHEESE DIP

280 g/10 oz package silken/soft tofu, well drained
2 tablespoons olive oil
2 scallions, sliced thin
2 tablespoons ricotta
1 tablespoon parmesan cheese
Juice of 1 lemon

Beat tofu in mixer or by hand until firm. Stir in remaining ingredients. Chill 2 hours.

Serve with salt-free crackers and raw fresh vegetables, such as carrot sticks, cauliflower and broccoli florets and cherry tomatoes.

CHEESEY SCRAMBLED EGGS

1 tablespoon unsalted margarine
4 tablespoons low-fat cottage cheese
4 spring onions, minced
1 clove garlic, pressed

4 eggs
Pepper

Melt margarine in frying pan. Add cottage cheese. Add onions and garlic. Sauté over low flame until browned. Increase heat to medium. Add beaten eggs and scramble until firm. Sprinkle pepper over top, and serve.

Note: For a higher-calcium variation, see Cheesey Scrambled Eggs below.

CHEESEY SCRAMBLED EGGS (HIGH CALCIUM)

1 tablespoon unsalted margarine
425 g/15 oz tofu
4 tablespoons low-fat cottage cheese
4 spring onions, minced
1 clove garlic, pressed
4 eggs
Pepper

Melt margarine in frying pan. Add tofu and cottage cheese, and mash together. Add onions and garlic. Sauté over low flame until browned. Increase heat to medium. Add beaten eggs and scramble until firm. Sprinkle pepper over top and serve.

CHEF'S SALAD (MEDIUM CALCIUM)

120 g/4 oz plain low-fat yogurt
2 teaspoons curry powder
4 hard rolls

    3 heads crisp lettuce
180 g/6 oz can of unsalted tuna, drained
1 slice Swiss cheese
120 g/4 oz unsalted (or low-salt) sliced turkey breast
2 medium tomatoes

Combine the yogurt and curry powder, and allow the flavours to mature.

Warm the rolls in the oven.

Wash and drain the greens, tear into large pieces, and place in four serving bowls. Flake the tuna onto the lettuce and toss. Slice the cheese and turkey breast into thin strips, and arrange on top of the lettuce. Cut the tomatoes into wedges and place on top of the other ingredients.

Add the curried yogurt dressing, or serve it separately. Serve the rolls with the salad.

Note: For higher- and lower-calcium variations, see Chef's Salad below.

CHEF'S SALAD (LOW CALCIUM)

    225 g/8 oz plain low-fat yogurt
2 teaspoons dill seed
4 hard rolls
3 heads crisp lettuce
180 g/6 oz can of tuna, drained
2 medium tomatoes
100 g/4 oz sliced turkey breast

Combine the yogurt and dill seed, and allow the flavours to mature.

Warm the rolls in the oven.

Wash and drain the greens, tear into large pieces, and place in four serving bowls. Flake the tuna onto the lettuce and toss. Cut the turkey breast into thin strips, and arrange on top of the lettuce. Cut the tomatoes into wedges and place on top of the other ingredients.

Add the dill seed dressing, or serve it separately. Serve the rolls with the salad.

Note: For higher-calcium variations, see Chef's Salad above and below.

CHEF'S SALAD (HIGH CALCIUM)

225 g/8 oz plain low-fat yogurt
2 tablespoons lemon juice
4 hard rolls
3 heads crisp lettuce
180 g/6 oz tuna, drained
2 medium tomatoes
4 slices Swiss cheese
120 g/4 oz sliced turkey breast

Combine the yogurt and lemon juice and allow the flavours to mature.

Warm the rolls in the oven.

Wash and drain the greens, tear into large pieces, and place in four serving bowls. Flake the tuna onto the lettuce and toss. Slice the cheese and turkey breast into thin strips, and arrange on top of the lettuce. Cut the tomatoes into wedges and place on top of the other ingredients.

Add the lemon yogurt dressing, or serve it separately. Serve the rolls with the salad.

CHERRY SAUCE WITH SORBET

  1 tablespoon fructose
  1 tablespoon cornflour
  500 ml/1 pt water
  1 teaspoon lemon juice
  450 g/1 lb fresh cherries, stoned and whole
  2 oranges, peeled and chopped
  600 ml/1 pt lemon sorbet
  125 ml/¼ pt warm brandy

In a cold saucepan, combine the fructose, cornflour and 250 ml/scant ½ pint of water, stirring briskly until the cornflour is dissolved. Bring to a boil and cook until thickened. Add the lemon juice, cherries and oranges. Simmer until the cherries are tender, adding additional water, if needed.

Serve over the lemon sorbet and top with warm brandy.

CHICKEN CASSEROLE

  225 g/8 oz fresh mushrooms
  125 ml/¼ pt semi-skimmed milk
  250 ml/½ pt water
  Pinch of oregano
  Pinch of basil
  1 teaspoon margarine
  4 skinless chicken breasts

Preheat oven to 350°F/180°C/Gas 4. Combine mushrooms, milk and water in a frying pan. Add oregano, basil and margarine. Cover and simmer for 10 minutes, stirring occasionally.

Place chicken breasts in a square baking pan. Cover each piece with one quarter of the mushroom mixture. Bake 1 hour, or until tender.

Note: For a higher-calcium version of this recipe, see Chicken Casserole below.

CHICKEN CASSEROLE (HIGH CALCIUM)

225 g/8 oz fresh mushrooms
125 ml/¼ pt semi-skimmed milk
250 ml/½ pt spring water
Pinch of oregano
Pinch of basil
1 teaspoon margarine
4 skinless chicken breasts
3 tablespoons parmesan cheese

Preheat oven to 350°F/180°C/Gas 4. Combine mushrooms, milk and water in a frying pan. Add oregano, basil and margarine. Cover and simmer for 10 minutes, stirring occasionally.

Place chicken breasts in a square baking pan. Cover each piece with one quarter of the mushroom mixture. Sprinkle with cheese. Bake 1 hour, or until tender.

CHICKEN IN YOGURT

4 tablespoons olive oil
4 chicken breasts, boned and skinned
Powdered ginger
Rosemary
225 g/8 oz plain low-fat yogurt

Rub olive oil on chicken breasts. Sprinkle lavishly with ginger and sparingly with rosemary. Place in shallow baking dish and cover with yogurt. Refrigerate 1 to 2 hours. Grill until golden brown, about 7 minutes. Bake at 350°F/180°C/Gas 4 uncovered for 50 minutes.

CHICKEN CHEDDAR CASSEROLE

4 chicken breasts
2 tablespoons margarine
1 tablespoon flour
250 ml/½ pt skimmed milk
120 g/4 oz cheddar cheese, grated
400 g/14 oz broccoli florets
Pinch of thyme
Pinch of sage

Preheat oven to 350°F/180°C/Gas 4. Wrap chicken in foil, place on a baking sheet, and bake about 1 hour.

Melt margarine in 1 litre (2 pint) saucepan, and make a roux with the flour. Stir in milk and cheese, and continue stirring until thick. Grease the bottom of a 1 litre (2 pint) casserole. Add broccoli. Remove chicken from oven, place on top of broccoli, and pour sauce over the top. Bake for 20 minutes. Sprinkle with herbs before serving.

CHICKEN KEBABS

4 large chicken breasts
2 teaspoons apple vinegar
¼ teaspoon cardamom
1 tablespoon lemon juice

2 tablespoons poultry seasoning
2 tablespoons sweet basil, finely ground
2 tablespoons sweet anise
6 tomatoes, skinned and cut in small chunks
10 slices of sweet white onion

Cut breasts into 12 square sections. Turn them in a mixture of vinegar, herbs and lemon juice. Slide chunks of chicken on skewer alongside tomato chunks and sliced onion. Place under grill, turning occasionally, for about 15 minutes.

CHICKEN IN PARMESAN CHEESE

30 g/1 oz bread crumbs, seasoned with 1 teaspoon sage, 1 teaspoon thyme, 1 teaspoon marjoram, pinch of basil, dash of oregano
6 tablespoons parmesan cheese, grated
1 clove of garlic, minced in garlic press
2 tablespoons corn oil
4 chicken breasts

Preheat oven to 350°F/180°C/Gas 4. Combine bread crumbs and cheese. Mix garlic into oil. Dip chicken in oil mixture, then roll in crumb mixture. Place on baking pan so that pieces are not touching. Bake 1 hour, or until tender.

CHICK PEAS, CELERY AND ONIONS

340 g/12 oz chick peas
1.5 l/2.75 pt water

1 tablespoon olive oil
2 stalks of celery hearts, cut fine
2 spring onions (complete), minced fine
Dash of pepper

Wash and soak chick peas overnight. Boil for 1–2 hours or until soft, but not mushy. Drain. Heat oil in frying pan. Sauté celery and onions. Toss with dash of pepper. Stir in the chick peas and serve at once.

CITRUS SORBET

400 g/14 oz fructose
1 litre/2 pts water
185 ml/6 fl oz lime, pink grapefruit or other citrus juice

Combine fructose and water and boil for 5 minutes. Add citrus juice. Cool, place in a plastic container and freeze. Serve with thin circles of peeled lime on top.

CLAMS IN TOMATO SAUCE

2 tablespoons olive oil
1 clove garlic, crushed
½ white onion, chopped fine
120 g/4 oz can tomatoes, puréed
1 can tomato paste
250 ml/½ pt water
180 g/6 oz clams, chopped
2 small salt-free crackers

Heat oil in saucepan. Add garlic and onion and sauté until onion is tender. Pour tomato purée into pan. Add water. Simmer for 15 minutes. Add clams and simmer 15 minutes more. Serve with crackers.

(For lunches, refrigerate sauce and pour into luncheon container.)

CODFISH (GRILLED)

4 cod fillets, about 450 g/1 lb
1 tablespoon olive oil
Juice of 1 lemon
2 cloves of garlic
1 teaspoon pepper
Dash of tarragon
Lemon wedges

Preheat the grill. Rinse fish under cold water and dry with paper towels. Make a paste of the oil, lemon juice, garlic, pepper and tarragon, and spread on the fish. Grill 3 to 5 minutes on each side. Serve with lemon wedges.

CODFISH (BAKED)

2 teaspoons safflower margarine
1½ lb cod, boned
Juice of 1 lemon
Dash of pepper
Dash of anise
500 g/18 oz plain low-fat yogurt

Preheat oven to 400°F/200°C/Gas 6. Grease baking dish

with margarine. Put cod in dish and sprinkle it with lemon juice, pepper and anise. Bake uncovered for 15–20 minutes. Spread yogurt over fish, then bake for another 10 minutes.

COMPOTE OF APPLES

4 apples, peeled and sliced thin
3 teaspoons clover honey
125 ml/¼ pt water
90 g/3 oz tofu, cut into ½-inch squares
1 teaspoon lemon juice
¼ teaspoon cinnamon
1 small lemon, sliced into ornamental crescents

Mix apples, honey and water thoroughly in a saucepan. Add the tofu gently and cook over a low flame. Cool. Spread lemon juice over the top, then sprinkle on the cinnamon. Chill. Serve with crescents of lemon on the side.

COURGETTE AND MUSHROOM SALAD

450 g/1 lb courgettes
450 g/1 lb mushrooms
2 tablespoons chives
Oregano
Basil
180 g/6 oz croutons
Juice of 1 lemon

Slice the vegetables, and mix with herbs and croutons. Squeeze lemon over them, and let stand for 15 minutes.

CREAM OF CHAMPAGNE SOUP

2 tablespoons margarine
1 large onion, chopped
1 tablespoon flour
350 ml/12 oz evaporated milk
750 ml/1¼ pts skimmed milk
225 g/8 oz broccoli
225 g/8 oz cauliflower
4 tablespoons sparkling wine
1 teaspoon basil
1 teaspoon oregano

Melt the margarine in a large saucepan and sauté the onion until brown and tender. Sprinkle on the flour and stir until dissolved. Gently add the evaporated milk and skimmed milk, stirring constantly over a low flame. Add broccoli and cauliflower. Simmer for 20 minutes, stirring occasionally. Add the sparkling wine, basil and oregano. Cover and cook for 5 minutes longer.

Place the vegetables and some of the liquid in a blender or food processor, and liquidize. Return the mixture to the pan and reheat. Serve hot.

EGG SALAD

2 eggs
200 g/7 oz long-grain rice
250 g/9 oz canned artichoke hearts in water
1 onion
2 cloves garlic
1 large tomato
½ teaspoon dry mustard

½ teaspoon basil
4 tablespoons olive oil
4 tablespoons lemon juice

Hard-boil the eggs, cool, peel and dice.

Cook the rice according to directions. Let cool to room temperature. Chop the onion and garlic, and cut the tomato into small pieces. Drain artichoke hearts.

Combine these ingredients, and sprinkle with the mustard and basil. Toss briefly with the oil and lemon juice. Serve at room temperature.

FETTUCCINE WITH TOFU

225 g/8 oz fettuccine
100 g/3½ oz tofu
180 g/6 oz low-fat ricotta
Small onion, chopped
2 cloves garlic, pressed
1 teaspoon worcestershire sauce
⅛ teaspoon pepper

Preheat oven to 350°F/180°C/Gas 4. Cook the noodles following package directions. Drain and mix with remaining ingredients. Pour into a greased 3-pint casserole. Bake uncovered for 30 minutes, or until a crust forms on top.

FETTUCCINE WITH TOMATOES AND PARMESAN CHEESE

450 g/1 lb tomatoes
3 tablespoons olive oil
2 cloves garlic

1 tablespoon basil
450 g/1 lb fettuccine
1 tablespoon parmesan cheese

Skin tomatoes and cut each one into 6 pieces. Discard seeds. Heat 1 tablespoon olive oil. Add garlic and basil. Sauté for 1 minute. Add tomatoes. Cook for 3 minutes more.

Prepare fettuccine as directed on package. Drain thoroughly. Warm 2 tablespoons of olive oil in a large frying pan. Place fettuccine in frying pan along with sauce. Cook over medium heat for 3 minutes, stirring occasionally. Transfer to a warm platter, sprinkle with parmesan cheese, and serve at once.

Note: For a higher-calcium variation, see Fettuccine with Tomatoes and Romano Cheese, below

FETTUCCINE WITH TOMATOES AND ROMANO CHEESE

450 g/1 lb tomatoes
3 tablespoons olive oil
2 cloves garlic
1 tablespoon basil
450 g/1 lb fettuccine
10 tablespoons romano cheese

Skin tomatoes and cut each one into six pieces. Discard seeds. Heat 1 tablespoon oil. Add garlic and basil. Sauté for 1 minute. Add tomatoes. Cook for 3 minutes more.

Prepare fettuccine as directed on package. Drain thoroughly. Warm 2 tablespoons of oil in a large frying pan. Place fettuccine in frying pan along with sauce. Cook over medium heat for 3 minutes, stirring occasionally. Transfer to a warm platter, sprinkle with romano cheese and serve at once.

FRESH FRUIT

4 fresh peaches, peeled and stoned
6 fresh apricots, peeled and stoned
8 cherries, stoned
8 slices fresh pineapple
2 bananas
3 tablespoons fructose
4 digestive biscuits
12 teaspoons triple sec (orange) liqueur
Mint leaves

Cut fruit into bite-size pieces, then sprinkle with fructose. Crush the biscuits and place at bottom of serving dishes. Spoon fruit on top. Add triple sec. Refrigerate for $1\frac{1}{2}$ hours until set. Serve cold, topped with mint leaves.

FRESH FRUIT SORBET

900 g/2 lb fruit, hulled or stoned
Juice of 1 lemon
250 ml/$\frac{1}{2}$ pt water
200 g/7 oz fructose

Place fruit in blender or food processor with half the lemon juice and purée. Boil the water, then add the fructose, cooking for 5 minutes. Stir in the purée and the rest of the lemon juice.

Cool, then place in plastic container and freeze.

FRUIT PARFAIT

2 tablespoons honey
Juice of ½ lemon
225 g/8 oz ricotta
120 g/4 oz tofu, cubed
340 g/12 oz fresh cherries and pineapple chunks

Mix honey, lemon and ricotta. In a large bowl, alternate layers of the ricotta mixture with the tofu and fruit. Make four layers. Chill well before serving.

FRUIT SALAD DRESSING

250 g/9 oz plain low-fat yogurt
340 g/12 oz clover honey
2 tablespoons grated onion
2 tablespoons celery seed
1 tablespoon dry mustard
1 teaspoon paprika
1 tablespoon lemon juice

Combine all ingredients. Refrigerate for 1 to 2 hours. Use as a dressing for fresh fruit salad.
    Yield: 625 ml/1 pt.

FRUIT SORBET

450 g/1 lb fruit purée
90 g/3 oz honey, clover or orange
250 ml/½ pt warm water
1 tablespoon lemon juice

Stirring constantly, combine honey and warm water. Add lemon juice and fruit purée. Freeze till firm.

GOURMET CHEESE DRESSING

225 g/8 oz low-fat ricotta
180 g/6 oz gorgonzola or blue cheese
2 tablespoons safflower oil
1 clove garlic
2 tablespoons lemon juice
1 tablespoon milk

Combine ricotta and gorgonzola or blue cheese. Add oil, garlic and lemon juice. Beat until well blended. Chill. Add milk. Refrigerate before serving.

Yield: 375 ml/13 fl oz.

GRILLED WHITE FISH

4 fillets white fish
1 tablespoon olive oil
4 teaspoons capers
1 lemon

Preheat grill for 2 minutes. Wash fish fillets under fresh cold water and dry with paper towel. Place on foil for grilling. Sprinkle with oil and capers. Squeeze whole fresh lemon on top of fish. Pieces of pulp may be added for tartness. Grill for 2 minutes; turn and grill for additional 2 minutes. Serve immediately.

HALIBUT STEAK WITH CAPERS

450 g/1 lb halibut steaks, 1 inch thick
Juice of 1 lemon
1 teaspoon margarine
4 tablespoons capers

Rinse the fish under running water and pat dry with a paper towel.

Sprinkle the lemon juice, margarine and capers on the fish. Grill at 6 inches below the flame, 5 minutes on each side. Serve immediately.

LASAGNE WITH PARMESAN CHEESE

2 tablespoons olive oil
2 cloves garlic, minced fine
2 medium-sized onions, diced
6 medium-sized tomatoes, skinned and cut in chunks
1 bay leaf
125 ml/¼ pt water
450 g/1 lb lasagne noodles
225 g/8 oz mozzarella cheese, sliced
180 g/6 oz ricotta cheese
6 tablespoons parmesan cheese
Dash of pepper

Grease an 8 × 8-inch baking dish with the oil.

Combine garlic, onion, tomato and bay leaf in a large covered saucepan. Simmer over very low heat for 1½ hours. Add water when sauce begins to thicken. Stir occasionally. Remove bay leaf.

Preheat oven to 350°F/180°C/Gas 4. Prepare lasagne noodles as directed on package, then drain thoroughly. Cover the bottom of the baking dish with one third of the lasagne noodles.

Top with half of the mozzarella cheese. Sprinkle with parmesan cheese and dash of pepper. Top with half the ricotta. Repeat layering process and top with final layer of lasagne. Spread the sauce over the top and sprinkle with parmesan cheese. Bake for 50 minutes. Let stand for 10 minutes, so lasagne can set in layers. Cut into 2-inch squares and serve.

LASAGNE (HIGH CALCIUM)

180 g/6 oz tofu
180 g/6 oz ricotta
1 teaspoon sweet basil
450 g/1 lb lasagne
400 g/4 oz tomatoes, puréed
225 g/8 oz cheese, sliced thin
120 g/4 oz part-skim mozzarella, sliced
120 g/4 oz mushroom caps, sliced

Preheat oven to 350°F/180°C/Gas 4. Combine the tofu and ricotta. Sprinkle with the basil.

Prepare the lasagne according to package directions and drain strips thoroughly. Coat a baking pan with nonstick spray, and spread one third of the tomato purée on the bottom. Add one third of the pasta and cover with some purée and one third of the cheese and mushrooms. Repeat twice, making three layers in all. Bake 45 minutes. Let stand for 10 minutes. Cut into 2-inch squares and serve.

LASAGNE

180 g/6 oz tofu
180 g/6 oz part-skim ricotta
1 teaspoon basil
450 g/1 lb lasagne
400 g/14 oz tomatoes, puréed
180 g/6 oz cheese, sliced thin
120 g/4 oz mushroom caps, sliced

Preheat oven to 350°F/180°C/Gas 4. Combine the tofu and ricotta. Sprinkle with the basil.

Prepare the lasagne according to package directions and drain strips thoroughly. Coat a baking pan with nonstick spray, and spread one third of the tomato purée on the bottom. Add one third of the pasta and cover with some purée and one third of the cheese and mushrooms. Repeat twice, making three layers in all. Bake 45 minutes. Let stand for 10 minutes. Cut into 2-inch squares.

Note: For a higher-calcium version of this recipe, see Lasagne above.

LINGUINE AND CAULIFLOWER

450 g/1 lb linguine
2 tablespoons olive oil
340 g/12 oz cauliflower florets
3 garlic cloves, crushed
90 g/3 oz ricotta, at room temperature
30 g/1 oz cheese, finely diced
2 tablespoons watercress, chopped

Prepare the linguine according to package directions and

drain thoroughly. Heat the oil in a large frying pan. Add the cauliflower and garlic. Sauté for 4 minutes. Cover frying pan and heat through for 3 more minutes. Drain the pasta and add it to the frying pan. Add the ricotta and mix well.

LINGUINE AND BROCCOLI

450 g/1 lb linguine
4 tablespoons virgin olive oil
450 g/1 lb broccoli florets, chopped into small pieces
4 cloves garlic, crushed
250 g/9 oz low-fat ricotta
2 tablespoons basil

Prepare pasta as directed on package and drain thoroughly. While pasta is cooking, heat 2 tablespoons of oil in a frying pan. Sauté the broccoli and garlic for 4 minutes. Cover and heat 4 minutes more. Stir in the ricotta and basil. Remove from heat. Place pasta in a large serving dish and sprinkle with 2 tablespoons of olive oil and basil. Mix, to prevent sticking. Pour contents of frying pan on top of pasta. Toss gently several times. Serve.

Note: For lower-calorie version of this recipe, see linguine and broccoli, below.

LINGUINE AND BROCCOLI

225 g/8 oz linguine
1 tablespoon virgin olive oil
450 g/1 lb broccoli florets
4 cloves garlic, crushed

250 g/9 oz part-skim ricotta
2 tablespoons basil

Prepare pasta as directed on package and drain thoroughly. While pasta is cooking, heat ½ tablespoon of oil in a frying pan. Sauté the broccoli and garlic for 4 minutes. Cover and heat 4 minutes more. Stir in the ricotta. Set on side of stove. Place pasta in a large serving dish. Sprinkle with ½ tablespoon of olive oil and the basil. Mix, to prevent sticking. Pour contents of frying pan on top of pasta. Toss gently several times. Serve.

MAYONNAISE

100 g/3.5 oz tofu
3 tablespoons low-fat yogurt
1 medium egg, boiled
2 teaspoons lemon juice
1 tablespoon spring onion, minced
Dash worcestershire sauce

Mix all ingredients in a blender and let stand 1 hour in refrigerator.

Yield: approximately 250 ml/½ pint.

MUSHROOMS AND PASTA

450 g/1 lb pasta (any shape)
4 tablespoons olive oil
450 g/1 lb mushrooms, sliced
4 cloves garlic, minced
225 g/8 oz pearl onions, whole

Pinch of thyme
Pinch of rosemary
Half a lemon

Cook the pasta according to package directions. Drain thoroughly.

Heat the oil and sauté the mushrooms, garlic, onions, thyme and rosemary until tender, but not mushy. Toss with the drained pasta. Squeeze the lemon over the mixture, and toss again briefly.

OMELETTE WITH TOFU AND CHEESE (HIGH CALCIUM)

60 ml/2 fl oz skimmed milk
4 eggs, slightly beaten
60 g/2 oz cheddar, grated
120 g/4 oz tofu, diced
2 tablespoons chives, chopped

Combine the eggs and milk, and pour into a nonstick frying pan. When partially set, cover with the cheese and tofu. Fold in half, remove to a serving dish, and sprinkle with chives.

OMELETTE WITH TOFU AND CHEESE

120 g/4 oz tofu, diced
4 eggs, slightly beaten
60 ml/2 fl oz skimmed milk
100 g/3.5 oz brie, cubed
1 tablespoon chives, chopped

Combine the eggs and milk, and pour into a nonstick frying pan. When partially set, cover with the cheese and tofu. Fold in half, remove to a serving dish, sprinkle with chives, and serve.

Note: For a higher-calcium version of this recipe, see Omelette with Tofu and Cheese, above.

OYSTER AND COD BAKE

4 tablespoons safflower oil
6 shallots, chopped fine
½ teaspoon green chilli powder
225 g/8 oz jar of oysters
50 g/1½ oz fresh bread crumbs, seasoned
675 g/1½ lb cod
Dash of pepper
Dash of tarragon
Dash of dill

Preheat oven to 400°F/200°C/Gas 6. Heat oil in frying pan. Add shallots and chilli and cook until soft. Dip oysters in crumbs, add to pan, and cook for 5 minutes. Place fish on a greased or nonstick baking pan and spread the oyster mixture over the fish. Sprinkle with pepper, tarragon and dill. Bake for about 30 minutes.

OYSTER SANDWICH

225 g/8 oz baguette french bread
450 g/1 lb jar oysters
3 tablespoons corn meal
2 tablespoons olive oil

4 teaspoons mayonnaise
20–40 drops hot pepper sauce (e.g. Tabasco)
Half a lemon

Warm the baguette in the oven, cutting it in half if necessary to fit. Lightly dredge the oysters with the corn meal, and allow them to dry briefly on a rack. Heat the olive oil in a heavy frying pan, adding up to 20 drops of hot pepper sauce to it, if desired. Cook the oysters briefly in the oil, no more than 2 minutes per side.

Slice the baguette in half horizontally. Spread the mayonnaise on the insides of both halves. Sprinkle hot pepper sauce on both halves. Place the oysters evenly along the bottom half. Squeeze the lemon juice over them, and then cover them with the top half of the bread. Cut the loaf into serving pieces, and serve immediately.

OYSTERS (GRILLED – HIGH CALCIUM)

225 g/8 oz french bread
225 g/8 oz low-fat yogurt
6 tablespoons skimmed milk
30 g/1 oz onion, chopped
1 clove garlic, minced
¼ teaspoon worcestershire sauce
225 g/8 oz canned smoked oysters

Slice the bread and brown it in a 350°F/180°C/Gas 4 oven for 10 minutes until crisp. Place the slices on a baking dish.

Blend the yogurt and milk, and fold in the remaining ingredients. Spoon onto the bread slices. Grill for about 3 minutes, or until slightly browned.

OYSTERS (GRILLED)

225 g/8 oz french bread
120 g/4 oz plain low-fat yogurt
180 g/6 oz water and oyster juice
30 g/1 oz onion, chopped
1 clove garlic, crushed
¼ teaspoon worcestershire sauce
225 g/8 oz canned smoked oysters

Slice the bread and brown it in a 350°F/180°C/Gas 4 oven for 10 minutes, until crisp. Place the slices on a baking dish.

Thin the yogurt with the water and oyster juice, and fold in the remaining ingredients. Spoon onto the bread slices. Grill for about 3 minutes, or until slightly browned.

Note: For a higher-calcium version of this recipe, see Oysters (Grilled) above.

PASTA WITH CHEESE

45 g/1½ onion, minced
2 tablespoons safflower margarine
60 g/2 oz soft bread crumbs
250 ml/½ pt ricotta sauce (see page 215)
120 g/4 oz pasta (any shape)
120 g/4 oz mozzarella or Bel Paese cheese

Preheat oven to 350°F/180°C/Gas 4. Grease a 3-pint casserole.

Sauté onion in margarine in a frying pan. Add half the bread crumbs and stir until brown. Set crumb mixture aside. Add ricotta sauce to mixture.

Boil pasta as instructed on packet and drain thoroughly. Place half of it in the greased casserole and cover with half of the crumb mixture. Repeat with the rest of the pasta and crumbs. Cover top with cheese and the remainder of the crumb mixture. Bake for 20 minutes, or until cheese is melted and crumbs are lightly browned.

PASTA WITH BROCCOLI

450 g/1 lb linguine
675 g/1½ lb broccoli
3 litres/6½ pts water
60 ml/2 fl oz olive oil
3 cloves garlic
Generous dash of pepper
4 tablespoons romano cheese

Cook linguine as directed on package. Drain thoroughly, saving three cups of the liquid.

Prepare broccoli tops, leaving only enough of the stems to secure the spears. Steam briefly, about 2 minutes. When finished, lay aside.

Heat olive oil in large saucepan. Sauté garlic until soft. Add broccoli and liquid. Season with pepper. Simmer over low heat for 10 minutes. Serve over linguine. Sprinkle with romano cheese.

PASTA WITH CORN AND HAM

180 g/6 oz pasta (any shape)
120 g/4 oz frozen corn kernels
200 g/7 oz cooked ham, diced

120 g/4 oz diced green chillies
200 g/7 oz green chilli salsa
1 large tomato

Cook the pasta and the corn according to package directions. Drain each and allow to cool.

Combine the ham, pasta and corn in a large serving bowl. Mix in the chillies and the salsa. Slice the tomato into wedges and arrange over the top of the mixture. Serve at room temperature.

PASTA WITH GARDEN VEGETABLES

225 g/8 oz sliced baby carrots
8 baby turnips
450 g/1 lb cooked tiny pasta shells
250 g/9 oz plain low-fat yogurt

Microwave the carrots and turnips for about 1 minute in a covered dish, or steam over water until tender but firm. Cool.

Mix with pasta and yogurt, and chill.

PASTA WITH MUSHROOMS, PIMIENTO AND CHEESE (HIGH CALCIUM)

90 g/3 oz mushrooms, sliced
225 g/8 oz pasta spirals, cooked
2 tablespoons pimiento, finely cut
225 g/8 oz cheddar cheese, cubed
250 ml/½ pt skimmed milk
1 small onion, chopped

Mustard to taste
1 teaspoon worcestershire sauce
1 teaspoon pepper
1 tomato, sliced

Steam the mushrooms and onion in a covered saucepan until soft. Mix with the pasta and pimiento and place in a nonstick 1 litre (2 pint) casserole.

Heat the cheese, milk, mustard, worcestershire sauce and pepper in a saucepan until the cheese melts. (This can be done in a microwave.) Stir half of the mixture into the pasta, and top with the tomato. Pour the rest of the mixture on top. Bake at 375°F/190°C/Gas 5 for 25 minutes, or until bubbly hot.

PASTA WITH MUSHROOMS, PIMIENTO AND CHEESE

90 g/3 oz mushrooms, sliced
225 g/8 oz cooked spiral pasta
2 tablespoons pimiento, finely cut
120 g/4 oz cheddar cheese, cubed
250 ml/½ pt skimmed milk
3 tablespoons garlic, chopped
1 teaspoon pepper
1 tomato, sliced

Steam the mushrooms and garlic in a covered saucepan until soft. Mix with the pasta and pimiento and place in a nonstick 1 litre (2 pint) casserole.

Heat the cheese, milk and pepper in a saucepan until the cheese melts. (This can be done in a microwave.) Stir half of the mixture into the pasta, and top with the tomato.

Pour the rest of the mixture on top. Bake at 375°F/190°C/Gas 5 for 25 minutes, or until bubbly hot.

Note: For a higher-calcium variation, see Pasta with Mushrooms, Pimiento and Cheese, above.

PASTA WITH CABBAGE AND SCALLIONS

450 g/1 lb egg noodles
2 tablespoons safflower margarine, melted
225 g/8 oz cabbage, sliced in thin sections
125 ml/¼ pt water
225 g/8 oz scallions, chopped fine

Cook noodles as directed on package. Drain. Warm oil in large frying pan. Sauté cabbage 3–4 minutes. Add water. Cover and simmer for 4 minutes. Place noodles on top of cabbage. Steam for 5 minutes.

Mix cabbage and noodles together and top with scallions. Serve at once.

PASTA SHELLS WITH TOMATO SAUCE

225 g/8 oz jumbo pasta shells
900 g/2 lb low-sodium tomato sauce
1 teaspoon basil
1 teaspoon oregano
560 g/1¼ lb silken/soft tofu
120 g/4 oz mozzarella cheese, shredded
120 g/4 oz parmesan cheese, grated

Preheat the oven to 350°F/180°C/Gas 4. Cook the pasta according to directions on the package. Drain.

Mix the tomato sauce with the basil and oregano. Line a 13 × 9 × 2-inch baking dish with half of the tomato sauce. Mix the tofu, mozzarella and parmesan. Place the cooked shells side by side in the pan in a single layer, and spoon the cheese mixture into them. Pour the remaining sauce over the shells. Bake for 30 minutes or until the shells are thoroughly heated.

PEACH BAKE

4 digestive biscuits, crushed
3 tablespoons safflower margarine, melted
6 large ripe peaches, pitted and cut in half
12 tablespoons wine or sherry
2 tablespoons lemon juice
2 tablespoons water
4 tablespoons fructose

Preheat oven to 375°F/190°C/Gas 5. Mix the crushed biscuits with the melted margarine, then line a shallow baking dish with the mixture. Place the peaches in the dish, cut side down. Combine the wine and lemon juice, pouring some over each half. Bake for a total of 30 minutes. After the first 15 minutes, pour the water over the peaches, to prevent scorching.

Five minutes before removing the dish from the oven, sprinkle the peaches with fructose. Serve warm.

PEACHES IN HONEY

4 large fresh peaches, peeled and cut into small chunks

　　180 g/6 oz orange honey
　　2 tablespoons lemon juice
　　Pinch of ginger

In serving dish combine all ingredients and let flavours blend for at least ½ hour. Serve at room temperature.

PEARS IN WINE

　　6 fresh pears
　　125 ml/¼ pt red wine
　　1 teaspoon cinnamon
　　90 g/3 oz clover honey
　　1 tablespoon lemon juice
　　Fresh mint sprigs

Peel and core the pears. Cut into lengthwise halves. In a double boiler, stir wine, cinnamon, honey and lemon juice for 1 minute. Gently add the pear halves, two at a time, and cook in sauce briefly, just until tender. Chill and serve topped with fresh mint.

PIZZA

　　450 g/1 lb fresh mushrooms
　　6 tablespoons olive oil
　　6 fresh tomatoes, skinned and cut into one-inch sections
　　2 cloves garlic, finely chopped
　　2 tablespoons oregano

2 tablespoons sweet basil
2 tablespoons capers
Dash of freshly ground black pepper
2 tablespoons parsley, chopped
8 crumpets

Trim the bottoms of the mushroom stems, then slice the mushrooms in half, lengthwise.

Sauté tomatoes in 4 tablespoons oil with garlic, oregano, sweet basil, capers, pepper and parsley for 15 minutes. Add mushrooms. Simmer 20 minutes more over low flame.

Preheat grill. Cut crumpets in half and place on oiled baking sheets, cut sides up. Top with tomato mixture.

Grill until warm and tomato sauce bubbles.

POPPYSEED DRESSING

340 g/12 oz orange honey
1 teaspoon dry mustard
160 ml/⅓ pt vinegar
3 tablespoons onion juice
2 tablespoons safflower oil
2 tablespoons lemon juice
3 tablespoons poppyseeds
2 tablespoons water, if necessary

Mix honey, mustard and vinegar. Stir in onion juice. Slowly add oil, beating constantly until thick. (You may also prepare in blender or food processor.) Stir in poppyseeds. Thin with water, if necessary.

Yield: 600 ml/1 pt.

RAVIOLI

120 g/4 oz bread crumbs, made from slightly stale french bread
450 g/1 lb chilled ricotta-filled ravioli (available at a delicatessen)
600 ml/1 pt skimmed milk
5 tablespoons parmesan cheese
2 tablespoons safflower oil

Preheat oven to 350°F/180°C/Gas 4. Sprinkle thin layer of bread crumbs evenly in bottom of deep pan. Dip ravioli into milk and place close together on top of breading. Repeat layers until pan is full. Sprinkle with parmesan cheese. Pour safflower oil on top. Bake until golden brown, about 20 minutes.

RED CABBAGE

1 red cabbage, cored and chopped
2 large apples, peeled, cored, and diced
1 tablespoon caraway seed
1 teaspoon malt vinegar
$\frac{1}{8}$ teaspoon pepper

Mix all ingredients. Simmer over low heat, stirring occasionally, for about 25 minutes.

RED SNAPPER WITH VEGETABLES

225 g/8 oz turnips
225 g/8 oz cucumber, peeled

225 g/8 oz mushrooms
450 g/1 lb broccoli
1 teaspoon cumin
2 teaspoons oregano
4 fillets red snapper (about 450 g/1 lb)
1 lime
4 sprigs fresh coriander leaves

Cut the turnips and cucumber into small cubes and place in a casserole. Rinse the mushrooms, slice and add. Trim the broccoli, separate into florets, and add. Sprinkle with cumin and oregano, and cover.

Rinse the fish under running water and pat dry with a paper towel. Half-fill a large frying pan with water and squeeze one quarter of the lime into it. Cut the remainder of the lime into four wedges. Measure the thickness of the fish. Place a large nonstick drip tray in the water, and place the fish fillets on it. Cover the fillets with the coriander leaves, and cover the pan. Bring the water to a boil, then turn down the heat and steam the fish for 10 minutes per inch of fish thickness.

Cook the vegetables in a microwave on high for about 4 minutes, or until tender but firm, or until you can smell the spices.

Apportion the vegetables on warmed plates, and place the fish on top. Garnish with lime wedges.

RICE PILAF

100 g/3.5 oz long grain white rice
250 ml/½ pint unsalted chicken stock (preferably homemade)
½ teaspoon thyme

½ teaspoon marjoram

Combine all ingredients, cover, and bring to a boil. Simmer 17 minutes. Let stand 10 minutes covered. Serve.

SALMON BAKE (HIGH CALCIUM)

450 g/1 lb canned salmon
1 egg, beaten
1 large onion, chopped
Juice of 1 lemon
250 g/9 oz ricotta
Marjoram
Thyme
Pepper
4 slices processed cheese

Preheat oven to 350°F/180°C/Gas 4. Blend the salmon in a bowl with the egg. Add the onion and juice of the lemon. Mix in the ricotta, herbs and pepper. Transfer mixture to a loaf tin or dish and top with the cheese. Bake for 40 minutes, covered. Remove cover and bake 10 minutes longer.

SALMON BAKE

450 g/1 lb canned salmon
1 egg, beaten
1 large onion, chopped

Juice of 1 lemon
125 g/4.5 oz low-fat ricotta
Marjoram
Thyme
Pepper
2 slices processed cheese

Preheat oven to 350°F/180°C/Gas 4. Blend the salmon in a bowl with the egg. Add the onion and the juice of the lemon. Mix in the ricotta, herbs and pepper. Transfer mixture to a loaf tin or dish and top with the cheese. Bake for 40 minutes, covered. Remove cover and bake 10 minutes longer.

Note: For a higher-calcium version of this recipe, see Salmon Bake above.

SALMON (GRILLED)

450 g/1 lb salmon steaks, 1 inch thick
Juice of ½ lemon
1 teaspoon olive oil
1 teaspoon oregano
1 teaspoon thyme
1 teaspoon basil
1 teaspoon rosemary

Rinse the fish under running water and pat dry with a paper towel. Sprinkle with lemon juice, olive oil and herbs, and grill the fish 6 inches below the flame for 5 minutes on each side. Serve immediately.

SALMON LOAF

450 g/1 lb canned salmon
250 ml/½ pt skimmed milk
1 egg beaten
3 tablespoons shallots, minced
2 teaspoons poultry seasoning
½ teaspoon tarragon
Corn oil margarine
Lemon wedges

Preheat oven to 375°F/190°C/Gas 5. Mix salmon and milk in a bowl. Add egg and remaining ingredients and mix well. Transfer the mixture to a loaf tin or dish greased with corn oil margarine. Bake for about 40 minutes.

Serve this aromatic seafood loaf garnished with lemon wedges. The delicate meat will give no hint that it has not come straight from the ocean to your kitchen.

SALMON MOULD

6-oz can pink salmon
450 g/1 lb cucumber, seeded and diced
30 g/1 oz onion, chopped fine
2 envelopes unflavoured gelatine
125 ml/¼ pt cold water
125 g/4.5 oz tomato purée
60 ml/2 fl oz cider vinegar
250 g/9 oz plus 2 tablespoons plain low-fat yogurt

Drain salmon, saving the liquid. Flake and mix the salmon with cucumber and onion. Soften gelatine in cold water. Combine salmon liquid, tomato purée and vinegar in a saucepan, and bring to a boil. Stir in the softened gelatine until dissolved. Blend this into the salmon mixture. Stir in 250 g/9 oz of yogurt.

Coat the inside of a 1 litre (2 pint) fish mould with 2 tablespoons yogurt, and fill with salmon mixture. Chill until firm. Unmould onto serving platter.

SAUCE RICOTTA

2 cloves garlic, crushed
4 tablespoons olive oil
340 g/12 oz low-fat ricotta
Juice of 1 large lemon, squeezed
2 teaspoons dry mustard
2 teaspoons wine vinegar
1 tablespoon mayonnaise
Dash of pepper

Sauté garlic in 2 tablespoons oil. Heat ricotta in double boiler. Add warm garlic and olive oil mixture and all other ingredients to the ricotta. Cook in double boiler for 15 minutes over medium-low flame, stirring occasionally. Serve at once over warm vegetables.

Note: Perfect for asparagus and broccoli. Adds a zesty flair to any vegetable. Also use as a replacement for white sauce.

SCALLOPS WITH YOGURT

1 teaspoon margarine
340 g/12 oz scallops
30 g/1 oz soft bread crumbs

$\frac{1}{8}$ teaspoon pepper
1 tablespoon anise
125g/4.5 oz plain low-fat yogurt

Coat the bottom of a square baking pan with the margarine. Wash the scallops, drain, and dry on paper towels. Cut the scallops in half if they are very large. Place half the scallops in the pan and cover with half of the bread crumbs, pepper and anise. Repeat. Pour the yogurt over the top and bake at 375°F/190°C/Gas 5 for 30 minutes.

SEAFOOD STRATA WITH CHEESE (HIGH CALCIUM)

280 g/10 oz package frozen shrimp, thawed
1 litre/2 pints skimmed milk
3 eggs
4 tablespoons sherry
1 tablespoon dry mustard
225 g/8 oz fresh crab meat
Margarine
6 slices slightly stale bread
120 g/4 oz parmesan cheese, grated

Quarter each slice of bread and dab with margarine. Mix shrimp, milk, eggs, sherry, mustard and crab meat. Grease casserole with margarine. Alternate layers of bread, cheese and shrimp mixture. Chill overnight or for a few hours. Bake at 350°F/180°C/Gas 4 for 1 hour.

SEAFOOD STRATA

280 g/10 oz package frozen shrimp, thawed
1 litre/2 pints skimmed milk
1 egg
4 tablespoons sherry
1 tablespoon dry mustard
225 g/8 oz fresh crab meat
Margarine
6 slices slightly stale bread

Quarter each slice of bread and dab with margarine. Mix shrimp, milk, egg, sherry, mustard and crab meat. Grease casserole with margarine. Alternate layers of bread with shrimp mixture. Chill overnight or for a few hours. Bake at 350°F/180°C/Gas 4 for 1 hour.

Note: For a higher-calcium version of this recipe, see Seafood Strata with Cheese, above.

SEA SALAD

400 g/14 oz small, cooked shrimp
200 g/7 oz crab meat, chopped
180 g/6 oz cucumber, chopped and seeded
½ teaspoon pepper
2 tablespoons onion, chopped
1½ teaspoons worcestershire sauce
Lettuce salad or 4 large tomatoes

Mix shrimp, crab meat, cucumber, pepper, onion and worcestershire sauce. Chill. Serve on lettuce or use to stuff tomatoes.

SHRIMP DIP

2 tablespoons safflower oil
1 tablespoon anchovy purée
1 tablespoon spring onion, minced
2 tablespoons tarragon vinegar
450 g/1 lb medium shrimp, cooked and chilled

Mix together the safflower oil, anchovy purée, onion and vinegar. Chill. Serve as a dip with the shrimp.

SHRIMP IN TOMATO BEDS

4 large, firm tomatoes
2 tablespoons olive oil
1 medium-size white onion, minced
280 g/10 oz cooked or canned shrimp
2 tablespoons basil
60 g/2 oz bread crumbs, seasoned with cheese
Dash of pepper
4 tablespoons parmesan cheese

Heat oven to 325°F/170°C/Gas 3. Slice off the top ends of the tomatoes, core the centres and turn upside down to permit them to dry. Heat the oil in a frying pan, add the onion and sauté until onion is shiny. Add the shrimp, basil, crumbs and pepper. Heat thoroughly. Fill the tomatoes with the mixture and sprinkle with cheese. Bake 15 minutes. Serve heated or chilled.

SHRIMP WITH DILL

450 g/1 lb shrimp
Fresh dill
4 slices French bread
1½ tablespoons chives
Pinch of pepper
60 g/2 oz plain low-fat yogurt
1 tablespoon lemon juice
1 tablespoon flour

Place the shrimp in cold water with fresh dill, bring to a boil and simmer 10 minutes.

Remove crusts from the bread and make bread crumbs. Mix in the chives.

Preheat the oven to 375°F/190°C/Gas 5. Drain the shrimp and let cool. Mix with the pepper, yogurt, lemon juice and flour, and place in a greased baking dish. Sprinkle the bread crumbs on top. Bake for 20 minutes.

SHRIMP BARBECUE

125 ml/¼ pint soy sauce
60 ml/2 oz olive oil
125 ml/¼ pt sherry
2 tablespoons lemon juice
1 teaspoon basil
1 teaspoon oregano
900 g/2 lb shrimp

Mix all ingredients except shrimp. Pour marinade over shrimp. Refrigerate for 3–4 hours. Thread shrimp on bamboo skewers and grill over coals or place under grill.

SHRIMP WITH PASTA

225 g/8 oz tiny pasta shells
2 tablespoons spring onions, chopped
1 slice lemon
1 bay leaf
1 litre/2 pts water
450 g/1 lb warm water shrimp, peeled and deveined
1 tablespoon olive oil
1 tablespoon flour
225 g/8 oz can tomatoes puréed
2 cloves garlic
1 tablespoon margarine

Cook pasta according to package directions. Drain. Place spring onions, lemon, bay leaf and water in a pot. Bring to a boil, add shrimp and simmer 5 minutes. Drain, reserving the liquid. Heat oil in a saucepan. Stir in reserved liquid and flour, tomato and garlic. Bring to a boil. Stir in shrimp and leave on flame until completely heated.

Toss pasta with margarine. Serve the shrimp over it.

SOLE (BAKED)

450 g/1 lb fillet of sole
2 tablespoons olive oil
Juice of 1 lemon
Fresh rosemary
Pepper

Preheat oven to 350°F/180°C/Gas 4. Rinse the fish under running water and pat dry with a paper towel. Grease a baking dish with 1 teaspoon of the oil. Combine the lemon juice, rosemary and pepper with the rest of the oil and marinate the fish in it for 2–4 hours. Remove from the marinade and place the fish in the baking dish. Bake for 35 minutes. If desired, garnish with additional fresh rosemary.

SPAGHETTI BOLOGNESE

900 g/2 lb tomatoes
450 g/1 lb fresh mushrooms
1 tablespoon olive oil
1–2 cloves garlic, diced
Pepper to taste
2–4 teaspoons oregano
2–4 teaspoons basil
450 g/1 lb spaghetti
½ cup grated parmesan cheese

Purée the tomatoes in a food processor or blender, or cut in a fine dice. Steam mushrooms until tender. Combine these ingredients in a pan, add the oil, garlic, pepper, oregano and basil, and cook covered for 30 minutes over low heat. Thin with water, if needed.

Cook the spaghetti and drain. Place on a serving dish and pour the sauce over it. Top with cheese.

SPAGHETTINI WITH CLAM SAUCE

60 ml/2 oz olive oil
2 cloves of garlic, crushed
½ tablespoon oregano
Dash of pepper

250 g/8 oz little neck clams, with juice
125 ml/¼ pt water
450 g/1 lb spaghettini

Heat oil in saucepan and sauté garlic, oregano and pepper. Add the clams with their water and cook until clams are tender, about 30 minutes. Add water, if necessary.

Prepare spaghettini as directed on package and drain thoroughly. Place spaghettini on warm platter and spoon clam sauce over it.

Note: For a higher-calcium version of this recipe, see Spaghettini with Clam Sauce below.

SPAGHETTINI WITH CLAM SAUCE (HIGH CALCIUM)

60 ml/2 oz olive oil
2 cloves of garlic, crushed
½ tablespoon oregano
Dash of pepper
250 g/9 oz little neck clams, with juice
125 ml/¼ pt water
450/1lb spaghettini
60 g/2 oz parmesan cheese

Heat oil in saucepan and sauté garlic, oregano and pepper. Add the clams with their water and cook until clams are tender, about 30 minutes. Add water, if necessary.

Prepare spaghettini as directed on package and drain thoroughly. Place spaghettini on warm platter and spoon clam sauce over it. Sprinkle with parmesan cheese.

STRAWBERRY MOULD

450 g/1 lb strawberries
120 g/4 oz fructose
125 ml/¼ pt sparkling wine
2 envelopes unflavoured gelatine
125 ml/¼ pt cold water
125 ml/¼ pt water, boiled
2 egg whites

Reserve a few strawberries with stems, for garnish. Hull the remainder of the strawberries and purée in a blender or food processor. Continue processing while adding fructose and sparkling wine. Place the mixture in a bowl and chill in the refrigerator.

Soften the gelatine in cold water, then add the hot water. Chill in the refrigerator till cool but not set.

Combine the gelatine and cold strawberries, beating until slightly thick and fluffy. Whip the egg whites until almost stiff, then fold into the fruit mixture.

Place in a 1.5 litre (3 pint) mould and refrigerate for 3½ hours. For serving, turn the mould out on a chilled platter and surround it with the reserved whole strawberries.

STUFFED EGGS

4 eggs, hard-boiled
120 g/4 oz canned, smoked sardines
2 tablespoons lemon juice
Pepper
Paprika
4 sprigs coriander leaves

Peel the eggs and halve lengthwise. Remove the yolks and mash with the sardines, lemon juice, pepper and paprika. Fill egg whites with the mixture. Garnish with additional paprika or whole coriander leaves.

TACOS (HIGH CALCIUM)

6 tomatoes, medium-sized
2 onions, medium sized, chopped
1 bouquet of coriander leaves, chopped
4 tablespoons olive oil
Dash of pepper
8 corn tortillas, medium-sized

Cut tomatoes into 1-inch cubes and sauté them with the onions and coriander leaves in 2 tablespoons oil for 15 minutes. Add pepper.

Lay tortillas on baking sheet. Place tomato mixture and cheese on centre of each. Fold into half-moon shapes. Heat the remaining oil in a frying pan and fry tortillas on both sides until crisp and brown. Drain on paper towels and serve immediately.

TACOS

8 corn tortillas, medium-sized
6 tomatoes, medium-sized
60 g/2 oz low-fat mozzarella cheese, sliced in thin segments
2 onions, medium sized, chopped
1 bouquet of coriander leaves, chopped
4 tablespoons olive oil
Dash of pepper

Cut tomatoes into 1-inch cubes and sauté them with the tomatoes, onions, and coriander leaves in 2 tablespoons oil for 15 minutes. Add pepper.

Lay tortillas on baking sheet. Place tomato mixture and cheese on centre of each. Fold into half moon shapes. Heat the remaining oil in a frying pan and fry tortillas on both sides until crisp and brown. Drain on paper towels and serve immediately.

Note: For a higher-calcium variation, see Tacos, above.

TOFU SHAKE

  280 g/10 oz soft tofu
  600 ml/1 pt skimmed milk
  60 g/2 oz fresh fruit
  2 tablespoons fructose
  1 tablespoon vanilla extract
  5 ice cubes

Place all ingredients in a blender and process until smooth and frothy.

Tofu comes in several types, and we have found that soft tofu is best for this shake.

TOFU CROQUETTES

  280 g/10 oz silken, firm tofu
  3 tablespoons flour
  Dash of pepper
  1 slightly beaten egg
  60 g/2 oz bread crumbs, seasoned with parmesan cheese

2 tablespoons olive oil
2 tablespoons worcestershire sauce
60 g/2 oz unsalted tomato purée
Lemon wedges

Slice tofu into croquette-size sections. Arrange slices between pieces of a thick paper towel to remove moisture. Mix flour and pepper. Dust tofu slices in flour mixture and drop into beaten egg. Sprinkle with bread crumbs. Heat oil in a large, shallow frying pan and sauté tofu wedges for 2 minutes on each side until crisp and golden. Blend worcestershire sauce and tomato paste. Pour mixture over tofu and serve with small lemon wedges.

TOMATO PURÉE

4 firm tomatoes, unpeeled
2 cloves garlic
3 tablespoons wine vinegar
2 tablespoons chives, chopped fine
2 tablespoons olive oil
1 small cucumber
4 tablespoons tomato purée
1 green chilli pepper, chopped fine
Dash of pepper

Purée all ingredients in a blender or food processor and serve chilled.

TROUT IN WINE SAUCE

1 tablespoon olive oil
6 shallots, chopped fine
1 tablespoon basil
2 bay leaves, crumpled
125 ml/¼ pt white wine
250 ml/½ pt water
450 g/1 lb rainbow trout, in 4 pieces

Heat oil and sauté the shallots. Add the bay leaves and basil. When the shallots are soft, add the wine and water, and simmer covered for 5 minutes. Place the trout in the mixture, cover, and cook for 10 minutes. Keep the heat high, but avoid boiling. Remove the fish to plates, and pour some of the sauce over it.

TUNA FILLETS IN WINE

1 tablespoon olive oil
450 g/1 lb tuna fillets
60 ml/2 fl oz dry white wine
½ medium onion, chopped
1 bay leaf, crushed
⅛ teaspoon pepper
1 teaspoon tarragon

Preheat oven to 350°F/180°C/Gas 4. Use a 1 litre (2 pint) shallow casserole. Brush casserole with oil, lay fish on bottom, and pour wine over it. Sprinkle other ingredients on top. Cover and bake for 30 minutes.

TURNIPS WITH TOMATOES

12 baby turnips
4 tomatoes, cut in wedges
4 teaspoons olive oil
8 tablespoons low-fat ricotta
8 tablespoons chopped chives

Quarter the turnips and microwave covered for 1 minute, or steam 5–10 minutes. Drain if necessary. Add tomato wedges and mix gently with oil. Cool. Mix with ricotta and chives. Chill.

VEGETABLE CAVIAR

4 small courgettes
1 tablespoon olive oil
2 small onions, chopped
1 tomato, chopped
225 g/8 oz cauliflower, chopped fine
225 g/8 oz broccoli florets, chopped
1 tablespoon lemon juice
½ teaspoon oregano
½ teaspoon basil
¼ teaspoon pepper

Slice the courgettes into rounds, then quarter the pieces. Heat the oil and sauté the courgettes with the onions, tomato, cauliflower, broccoli, lemon juice, herbs and pepper. Mix thoroughly. Let cool slightly before serving.

Note: For a higher-calcium version of this recipe, see Vegetable Caviar, below.

VEGETABLE CAVIAR (HIGH CALCIUM)

4 small courgettes
1 tablespoon olive oil
2 small onions, chopped
1 tomato, chopped
225 g/8 oz cauliflower, chopped fine
225 g/8 oz broccoli florets, chopped
1 tablespoon lemon juice
½ teaspoon oregano
½ teaspoon basil
¼ teaspoon pepper
280 g/10 oz tofu, diced
225 g/8 oz plain low-fat yogurt

Slice the courgettes into rounds, then quarter the pieces. Heat the oil and sauté the courgettes with the onions, tomato, cauliflower, broccoli, lemon juice, herbs and pepper. Mix thoroughly. Let cool slightly, then add the tofu and yogurt.

VEGETABLE LOAVES

425 g/15 oz tofu, drained
1 clove garlic, chopped
1 tablespoon fresh chives, or finely chopped bread crumbs, seasoned with oregano and basil
1 beaten egg
Pinch of black pepper
1 tomato, puréed
1 teaspoon oregano
1 teaspoon basil (optional)
2 tablespoons romano cheese, grated

Preheat oven to 350°F/180°C/Gas 4. Blend tofu, garlic, chives, seasoned crumbs, egg and pepper. Mould into 1½-inch diameter balls. Place the balls in a greased, nonstick pan and sauté until crisp-looking. Transfer them to a loaf tin, pour tomato purée over them and sprinkle with oregano (and basil) and grated cheese. Bake for 15 minutes. Serve hot or cold, or with spaghetti.

VEGETABLE-YOGURT LOAF (HIGH CALCIUM)

2 cloves garlic, crushed
2 tablespoons fresh chives, finely chopped
10 mushrooms, thinly sliced
2 tomatoes, thinly sliced
340 g/12 oz plain low-fat yogurt
560 g/1¼ lb tofu, cut in ½-inch cubes
60 g/2 oz parmesan

Preheat oven to 350°F/180°C/Gas 4. Sauté garlic and chives in a lightly greased, nonstick pan until tender. Combine with mushrooms and tomatoes in a bowl and mix gently. Place half of the mixture on the bottom of a greased, nonstick loaf tin. Pour half of the yogurt on top and add a layer of half the tofu. Pour one quarter of the yogurt over the tofu. Layer balance of ingredients in the same sequence. Bake for 30 minutes.
Serve with the parmesan.

VEGETABLE-YOGURT LOAF

2 cloves garlic, crushed
2 tablespoons fresh chives, finely chopped

    10 mushrooms, thinly sliced
    2 tomatoes, thinly sliced
    180 g/6 oz low-fat yogurt
    280 g/10 oz tofu, cut in ½-inch cubes

Preheat oven to 350°F/180°C/Gas 4. Sauté garlic and chives in a lightly greased, nonstick pan until tender. Combine with mushrooms and tomatoes in a bowl and mix gently. Place half of the mixture on the bottom of a greased, nonstick loaf tin. Pour half of the yogurt on top and add a layer of half the tofu. Pour one quarter of the yogurt over the tofu. Layer balance of ingredients in the same sequence. Bake for 30 minutes.

Note: For a higher-calcium version of this recipe, see Vegetable-yogurt Loaf, above.

VEGETABLES WITH NOODLES

    450 g/1 lb egg noodles
    225 g/8 oz mange tout
    340 g/12 oz bean-sprouts
    180 g/6oz can water chestnuts, drained
    120 g/4 oz cucumber, chopped fine and seeded
    120 g/4 oz grated carrots
    225 g/8 oz tofu
    2 tablespoons olive oil
    4 small spring onions, chopped fine

Cook noodles as directed on the package and drain. Cook all the vegetables in a steamer until almost tender. Dice the tofu into ½-inch cubes. Heat the oil in a frying pan and add the vegetables and tofu. Cook over a low flame just until hot.

Place the noodles on a serving dish, cover with the vegetables, and serve immediately.

VERMICELLI WITH TOMATO SAUCE

6 tomatoes, medium-sized
450 g/1 lb vermicelli (sometimes called fidelini)
2 cloves garlic, crushed
2 onions, medium-sized, diced
1 tablespoon oregano
1 tablespoon basil
4 tablespoons olive oil

Bring water to a boil and immerse tomatoes for a few seconds to make it easy to remove skins. Cut the tomatoes into 2.5 cm/1 inch cubes.

Cook vermicelli as instructed on package and drain thoroughly.

Sauté the garlic, onion, oregano and basil in the oil in a large frying pan. Add tomatoes and cook over medium heat for 15 minutes, stirring occasionally, but avoid mashing tomatoes.

Serve pasta on a heated platter topped with sauce.

Note: For a higher-calcium version of this recipe, see Vermicelli with Tomato Sauce and Cheese, below.

VERMICELLI WITH TOMATO SAUCE AND CHEESE

6 tomatoes, medium-sized
450 g/1 lb vermicelli (sometimes called fidelini)
2 cloves garlic, crushed

2 onions, medium-sized, diced
1 tablespoon oregano
1 tablespoon basil
4 tablespoons olive oil
8 tablespoons parmesan cheese

Bring water to a boil and immerse tomatoes for a few seconds to make it easy to remove skins. Cut the tomatoes into 2.5 cm (1 inch) cubes.

Cook vermicelli as instructed on package and drain thoroughly.

Sauté the garlic, onion, oregano and basil in the oil in a large frying pan. Add tomatoes and cook over medium heat for 15 minutes, stirring occasionally, but avoid mashing tomatoes.

Serve pasta on a heated platter topped with sauce and sprinkled with parmesan cheese.

WHIPPED DELIGHT

425 g/15 oz tofu
3 tablespoons orange honey
2½ teaspoons vanilla extract

Blend all ingredients until smooth. Serve as topping on fruit.

A CALCIUM COUNTER OF ABSORBABLE (USABLE) CALCIUM

The Calcium Counter lists basic foods alphabetically so that you can quickly look up the calcium content of many foods. To work out the calcium content in a prepared food, such as apple pie, look up the separate ingredients – the amount of apples, sugar, flour, etc. in a serving – and add up the calcium amounts. If you calculate it directly from the table, it will be much more accurate than if we try to measure it for you because recipes and portion sizes vary widely. Don't rely on calcium counters published in other books. All such counters report the *total* calcium in a food or recipe, rather than the usable calcium, or calcium that the body is able to absorb. In a given food, much of the reported calcium may be completely unusable, making your calcium count woefully inaccurate.

Most people tend to eat the same things repeatedly. Once you calculate the calcium content of your favourite prepared foods, write them in a notebook or diary and you won't have to do the calculations again.

By picking high-calcium sources and varying the food groups, you can put together a balanced high-calcium diet of your own. There are some foods for which data on compounds that bind calcium are unavailable, and these are marked with an asterisk (*).

Food	True calcium available mg per 100 g	Calories	% fat
Abalone * (tuna)	37	98	1
Albacore (tuna)	26	177	8
Almonds, dried	−33	598	54
Anchovy, pickled	168	176	10
Apple juice, bottled	1	47	0
Apples	7	58	1
Apple sauce *	4	91	0
Apricots	14	86	0
Artichokes	47	26	0
Asparagus	20	20	0
Avocados	10	167	16
Bacon, back	14	277	18
Bacon, streaky	14	611	52
Baking powder, scones	121	369	17
Bamboo shoots	13	27	0
Bananas	8	85	0
Barley	−90	348	1
Beans, canned, red kidney	16	90	0
Beans, broad	47	111	1
Beans, mung *	17	28	0
Beans, runner *	50	22	0
Beans, young, green in pod	−20	25	0
Beef, corned, medium fat	20	216	12
Beef, rump, roasted	10	317	23
Beer, 4.5% alcohol, 8 oz	−20	42	0
Beetroot	−34	32	0
Biscuits, sweet	37	480	20
Blackberries	24	58	1
Blueberries	8	62	1
Bran, wheat	−350	240	3
Brazil nuts	−198	654	67
Bread, French	43	290	3
Bread, white	68	269	3
Bread, whole-wheat	33	241	3

Food	True calcium available mg per 100 g	Calories	% fat
Broccoli	103	32	0
Brussels sprouts	33	36	0
Brussels sprouts, boiled	31	45	0
Bulgur (parboiled wheat)	−35	182	3
Burbot	0	82	1
Butter	20	716	81
Butterfish	0	169	10
Buttermilk	121	36	0
Cabbage, green	49	24	0
Cabbage, red	39	31	0
Cabbage, savoy *	65	24	0
Cantaloupe *	13	30	0
Carp	50	115	4
Carrots, boiled	26	31	0
Carrots, raw	31	42	0
Casaba melon *	14	27	0
Cauliflower	20	22	0
Caviar, sturgeon	276	262	15
Celery	34	17	0
Chard, Swiss	−220	25	0
Cheese, processed	697	370	30
Cheese, blue or Roquefort	315	368	31
Cheese, Brie	185	300	23
Cheese, Camembert	105	299	25
Cheese, Cheddar	750	398	32
Cheese, cottage, full-fat	94	106	4
Cheese, cottage, low-fat	90	86	0
Cheese, cream	62	374	38
Cheese, Edam	739	354	26
Cheese, feta	500	262	20
Cheese, fontina	557	385	29
Cheese, goat	405	426	28
Cheese, Gouda	707	354	26
Cheese, Gruyère	1,025	410	30

Food	True calcium available mg per 100 g	Calories	% fat
Cheese, Limburger	590	354	28
Cheese, mozzarella	525	280	20
Cheese, mozzarella (low-moisture, low-fat)	739	276	16
Cheese, Muenster	725	364	28
Cheese, Neufchatel	75	259	22
Cheese, Parmesan	1,140	393	26
Cheese, provolone	764	350	25
Cheese, romano	1,078	385	25
Cheese, ricotta (low-fat)	295	149	9
Cheese, ricotta (whole-milk)	207	189	13
Cheese, Swiss	925	370	28
Cherries	19	70	0
Chestnuts *	17	194	2
Chicken, roasted	10	290	20
Chick peas	150	360	5
Chilli con carne, with beans	32	133	6
Chilli con carne, without beans	38	200	15
Chives	69	28	0
Chocolate, milk, 3.5% fat	111	85	4
Chop suey, with meat	35	62	3
Chow mein, chicken	23	102	4
Clams, canned	55	52	1
Clams, raw	69	80	1
Coconut	−37	346	35
Cod	10	78	0
Coffee, cup, regular	−10	0	0
Coleslaw, with mayonnaise	44	144	14
Corn, sweet	1	96	1
Cornflakes	8	386	0
Cowpeas (blackeyed peas)	24	108	1
Crab, canned	45	101	3
Crab, devilled	47	188	9

Food	True calcium available mg per 100 g	Calories	% fat
Crab, steamed	43	93	2
Crackers, plain	40	384	9
Crackers, salted	21	433	12
Crackers, soda	22	439	13
Cranberries *	14	46	1
Cranberry juice cocktail *	5	65	0
Cranberry sauce, sweetened	6	146	0
Crayfish	77	72	1
Cream puffs with custard	81	233	14
Cream, single	108	134	12
Cream, whipping	85	300	31
Crisps	40	568	40
Cucumbers	25	15	0
Currants, black *	58	54	0
Currants, red and white *	28	50	0
Custard, baked	112	115	6
Dates *	59	274	1
Doughnuts, cake-type	40	391	19
Duck	10	326	29
Eclair	80	239	14
Eel, raw	18	233	18
Egg	54	163	12
Eggplant	8	25	0
Elderberries *	38	72	1
Endive and chicory	80	20	0
Fennel, leaves	98	28	0
Figs, dried *	126	274	1
Figs, fresh	35	80	0
Flounder, baked	23	202	8
Frog legs	18	73	0
Fruit cocktail	9	76	0
Garlic, clove	27	137	0
Ginger, root *	23	49	1
Goose, roasted	11	426	36

Food	True calcium available mg per 100 g	Calories	% fat
Gooseberries	− 6	39	0
Grapefruit, all types	15	41	0
Grapefruit juice, all types	9	39	0
Grapejuice, bottled	9	66	0
Grapes, white	5	67	0
Guavas ★	23	62	1
Haddock, fried	40	165	6
Halibut, broiled	16	171	7
Ham, medium fat, roasted	10	374	31
Herring, canned	147	208	14
Honey	5	304	0
Horseradish (1 oz)	40	87	0
Ice cream (10% fat)	146	193	11
Jams and preserves	20	272	0
Jellies	21	273	0
Kale	176	38	1
Kidneys, beef, braised	17	252	12
Kohlrabi ★	40	29	0
Kumquats ★	63	65	0
Lake herring	12	96	2
Lamb, leg, roasted	10	279	19
Lard	0	902	100
Leeks	32	52	0
Lemon juice	6	25	0
Lemons, peeled fruit	26	27	0
Lentils, dry	− 14	340	1
Lettuce, butterhead	35	14	0
Lime juice ★	9	26	0
Limes ★	33	28	0
Liquor, hard (1.5 fl oz)	− 15	263	0
Liver, calves, fried	9	229	11
Lobster	87	194	11
Lobster salad	36	110	6
Lobster, northern	65	95	2

Food	True calcium available mg per 100 g	Calories	% fat
Loganberries *	35	62	1
Loquats *	20	48	0
Lychees *	8	64	0
Macaroni cheese	83	95	4
Macaroni, cooked	10	148	1
Mackerel, Atlantic, raw	5	191	12
Mangos *	10	66	0
Maple syrup *	104	252	1
Margarine	20	720	81
Marmalade, citrus	32	257	0
Milk, butter (8 oz)	277	82	0
Milk, evaporated	252	137	8
Milk, semi-skimmed (8 oz)	273	125	2
Milk, skimmed (8 oz)	277	90	0
Milk, whole, 3.5% fat (8 oz)	270	160	4
Muffins, plain	104	294	10
Mushrooms	5	28	0
Mussels	88	95	2
Mustard greens	183	31	1
Mustard, prepared ($\frac{1}{2}$ oz)	18	91	6
Nectarines *	4	64	0
Noodles, egg	10	125	2
Oatmeal, cooked	− 17	55	1
Ocean perch	20	88	1
Octopus	29	73	1
Oil, cooking	0	884	100
Okra	26	36	0
Olives *	61	116	13
Onions *	25	38	0
Orange juice	10	48	0
Oranges	38	49	0
Oysters	94	66	2
Pancakes	101	231	7
Papayas */paw paw	20	39	0

Food	True calcium available mg per 100 g	Calories	% fat
Parsley	164	44	1
Parsnips	30	76	1
Passion fruit *	13	90	1
Peaches	9	38	0
Peanut butter	− 163	581	49
Peanuts, roasted	− 163	581	49
Pears	5	61	0
Peas, boiled	22	43	0
Peas, green, baby, boiled	18	71	0
Pecans	− 19	687	71
Peppers, chilli, green	6	37	0
Persimmons, raw	27	127	0
Pickles, cucumbers, dill	26	11	0
Pickles, relish, sweet	20	138	1
Pie, apple	8	256	11
Pie, banana custard	66	221	9
Pineapple, fresh *	17	52	0
Pineapple, heavy syrup *	10	74	0
Pineapple juice *	15	55	0
Pizza, with cheese	156	245	7
Plums, damson *	13	66	0
Pomegranate *	3	63	0
Popcorn, oil and salt added	8	456	22
Pork, loin, grilled	11	391	32
Potatoes, baked	9	93	0
Potatoes, boiled	2	76	0
Pretzels	22	390	5
Prune juice, bottled *	14	77	0
Prunes *	48	255	1
Pumpkin *	25	33	0
Radishes *	30	17	0
Raisins *	62	289	0
Raspberries, black	26	73	1
Rhubarb	− 148	16	0

Food	True calcium available mg per 100 g	Calories	% fat
Rhubarb, cooked, with sugar	− 125	141	0
Rice pudding with raisins ★	98	146	3
Rice, white, cooked	− 1	109	0
Roe, cod or shad, baked	13	126	3
Rolls, plain (pan rolls)	74	298	6
Rusk ★	20	419	9
Salad dressing, blue cheese	81	504	52
Salad dressing, French	11	410	39
Salad dressing, Italian	10	552	60
Salad dressing, mayonnaise	18	718	80
Salad dressing, Russian	19	494	51
Salad dressing, thousand island	11	502	50
Salmon	79	217	13
Sapotes (marmalade, plums) ★	39	125	1
Sardines, in oil	354	311	24
Sardines, in tomato sauce	448	197	12
Sauerkraut, canned ★	36	18	0
Scallops, bay and sea, steamed	115	112	1
Shallots	37	72	0
Shrimp	215	106	1.8
Soybeans, boiled	73	130	6
Spaghetti, cooked	10	148	1
Spinach	− 166	23	0
Squash, summer, boiled	15	14	0
Strawberries	16	37	1
Sugar, white, granulated	0	385	0
Swede	55	35	0
Sweet potatoes, baked	14	141	1
Swordfish	19	174	6
Swordfish, grilled	27	118	4
Tangerine juice ★	18	43	0
Tangerines ★	40	46	0

Food	True calcium available mg per 100 g	Calories	% fat
Tea, brewed 2 minutes (8-oz cup)	−20	2	0
Tea, brewed 4 minutes (8-oz cup)	−40	2	0
Tea, brewed 6 minutes (8-oz cup)	−60	2	0
Tofu, firm	159	87	5
Tofu, silken	94	53	3
Tomato juice	5	19	0
Tomato purée *	13	39	0
Tomatoes, raw	12	22	0
Tomato sauce	22	106	0
Turnips	34	23	0
Walnuts	−59	651	64
Watercress	146	19	0
Watermelon *	7	26	0
Wheat germ	−50	363	11
Wheat, shredded	−157	354	2
Whitefish	22	155	7
Wine, 12.2% alcohol	8	85	0
Yam, raw	20	101	0
Yogurt, fruit, low-fat (8 oz)	305	204	1
Yogurt, plain, low-fat (8 oz)	411	119	1

Note for professionals: This calcium counter is an educational tool to help in selection of foods that will maximize absorption of calcium. There are two common compounds in food that interfere with calcium absorption: phytic acid and oxalic acid. A group of scientists, including Dr June L. Kelsay of the nutritional research centre of the US Department of Agriculture and Dr John W. Erdman Jr of the University of Illinois at Urbana, have been studying the effects of these acids on calcium absorption. They have provided valuable advice used in calculation of this table.

We have generally assumed that one mole of oxalic acid binds one mole of calcium, and one mole of phytic acid binds three moles of calcium. These assumptions are supported by several clinical studies of unadapted individuals.

Exposure to compounds that bind calcium tends to be episodic in individuals consuming a varied western diet, so there is relatively little opportunity for adaption over the long term. Adaption may also be limited at the low levels of calcium intake present in much of the population.

* Foods marked with an asterisk have not been fully analysed for phytate and/or oxalate content in the open literature, and the true calcium content is our best estimate from available data.

DRINKING WATER IN MAJOR UK CITIES

Calcium content of water throughout the United Kingdom varies considerably. The first column gives estimated contents of calcium in milligrams per litre, calculated using data on water hardness from water authorities. The higher the value, the greater the calcium content of your water. The second column gives sodium content, also in milligrams per litre. Healthy water has a sodium content of less than 50 milligrams per litre. However, the figures are intended only as a guide. Calcium content varies considerably between different areas of a city – water supplies to consumer taps are sometimes mixed from several different sources. If you want to find out exactly the calcium and sodium content of your water, you may wish to contact one of the ten water authorities; in Scotland, the Regional Councils; and in Northern Ireland, the Department of the Environment water service divisions. Ask for scientific services. Addresses and telephone numbers are given below.

Town/city	Estimated average calcium content (milligrams per litre)	Average sodium content (milligrams per litre)
North East		
Durham	16	6
Tyneside	35	20
Newcastle	47	NA
Hartlepool	126	NA

Town/city	Estimated average calcium content (milligrams per litre)	Average sodium content (milligrams per litre)
North West		
Liverpool	7–38	3
Manchester	4–13	5
Preston	11	7
Lancaster	8	5
Kendal	8	4
Carlisle	10	6
Yorkshire		
Harrogate	16	NA
Hull	83–125	NA
York	96	NA
Sheffield	22–58	NA
Leeds	83	NA
Doncaster	77	NA
Midlands		
Nottingham	42	NA
Worcester	49	NA
Newcastle under Lyme	68	NA
Stoke on Trent	38	NA
East Anglia		
Bedford	111	NA
Bury St Edmunds	113	NA
Grimsby	82	NA
Ipswich	116	NA
Lincoln	85	NA
Northampton	68	NA
Peterborough	100	NA
South East		
Guildford	57	14
Oxford	95	22
Banbury	80	32

Town/city	Estimated average calcium content (milligrams per litre)	Average sodium content (milligrams per litre)
Reading	110	14
Swindon	98	7–29
Greater London	89	26
Gravesend	64	NA
Thanet	90	NA
South		
Isle of Wight	65	NA
Southampton	85	NA
Brighton	80	NA
Winchester	86	NA
Poole	51–96	8–48
South West		
Bath	74–128	3–80
Bristol	69–84	NA
Bridgewater	10–128	4–33
Taunton	10–128	4–33
Yeovil	10–128	4–33
Plymouth	8	7
Exeter	21	10
Scotland		
Edinburgh	8–35	6
Glasgow	4	3
Inverness	9	8
Wales		
Cardiff	6–42	NA
Carmarthen	8–62	NA
Colwyn Bay	3–42	NA
Meirionydd	5–19	NA
Merthyr Tydfil	6–11	NA
Monmouth	30	NA
Neath	6–27	NA
Newport	8–42	NA
Swansea	6–64	NA

Town/city	Estimated average calcium content (milligrams per litre)	Average sodium content (milligrams per litre)

Northern Ireland

| Belfast | 13–38 | 5–15 |
| Londonderry | 20 | 20 |

England and Wales

ANGLIAN WATER
Ambury Road,
Huntingdon PE16 6NZ.
Telephone: Huntingdon (0480) 56171

NORTHUMBRIAN WATER
Regent Centre, Gosforth,
Newcastle upon Tyne, NE3 3PX.
Telephone: Tyneside (091) 28243151

NORTH-WEST WATER
Dawson House, Great Sankey,
Warrington WA5 3LW.
Telephone: Penketh (092 572) 4321

SEVERN TRENT WATER
Abelson House, 2297 Coventry Road
Sheldon, Birmingham B26 3PU.
Telephone: 021 743 4222

SOUTHERN WATER
Guildbourne House, Worthing,
West Sussex BN11 1LD.
Telephone: Worthing (0903) 205252

SOUTH-WEST WATER
Peninsula House, Rydon Lane,
Exeter EX2 7HR.
Telephone: (0392) 219666

THAMES WATER
Nugent House, Vastern Road,
Reading RG1 8DB.
Telephone: Reading (0734) 593333

WELSH WATER
Cambrian Way, Brecon
Powys LD3 7HP.
Telephone: Brecon (0874) 3181

WESSEX WATER
Wessex House, Passage Street,
Bristol, Avon BS2 0JQ.
Telephone: Bristol (0272) 290611

YORKSHIRE WATER
West Riding House, 67 Albion Street
Leeds LS1 5AA.
Telephone: Leeds (0532) 448201

Scotland

BORDERS REGIONAL COUNCIL
Regional Headquarters,
Newtown St Boswells TD6 0SA.
Telephone: St Boswells (0835) 23301

**Directorate of Water and Drainage Services,
West Grove, Waverley Road,
Melrose, Roxburghshire TD6 9SJ.
Telephone: Melrose (089682) 2056**

CENTRAL REGIONAL COUNCIL
Viewforth, Stirling FK8 2ET.
Telephone: Stirling (0786) 73111

**Water and Drainage Department,
Woodlands, St Ninians Road,
Stirling FK8 2HB.
Telephone: Stirling (0786) 64213
and 62811**

DUMFRIES AND GALLOWAY REGIONAL COUNCIL
Council Offices, Dumfries DG1 2DD
Telephone: Dumfries (0387) 53141
**Water & Sewerage Department,
70 Terregles Street,
Dumfries DG2 9BB.
Telephone: Dumfries (0387) 63011**

FIFE REGIONAL COUNCIL
Fife House, North Street,
Glenrothes, Fife KY7 5LT.
Tel: Glenrothes (0592) 754411

**Department of Engineering,
Fife House, North Street,
Glenrothes, Fife KY7 5LT.
Telephone: Glenrothes (0592) 754411**

GRAMPIAN REGIONAL COUNCIL
Woodhill House, Ashgrove Road West,
Aberdeen AB9 2LU.
Telephone: 0224 682222
Telex: 739277

HIGHLAND REGIONAL COUNCIL
Regional Buildings, Glenurquhart Road
Inverness IV3 5NX.
Telephone: 0463 234121
Telex: 75313
Fax: 0463 223201

LOTHIAN REGIONAL COUNCIL
Regional Headquarters,
George IV Bridge,
Edinburgh EH1 1UO.
Tel: Edinburgh (031) 229 9292
Telex: 727586

**Department of Water and Drainage,
8 Cockburn Street,
Edinburgh EH1 1NZ.
Telephone: Edinburgh (031) 229 9292**

STRATHCLYDE REGIONAL COUNCIL
Strathclyde House, 20 India Street,
Glasgow G2 4PF.
Telephone: 041 227 3261

**Water Department,
419 Balmore Road,
Glasgow G22 6NU.
Telephone: 041 336 5333
Sewerage Department,
20 India Street, Glasgow G2 4PF.
Telephone: 041 227 3721
Telex: 777237**

TAYSIDE REGIONAL COUNCIL
Tayside House, 26–28 Crichton St.,
Dundee DD1 3RA.
Telephone: 0382 23281

**Water Services Department,
Bullion House, Invergowrie,
Dundee DD2 5BB.
Telephone: Dundee (0382) 562581
Telex: 76518-TAYREG**

ORKNEY ISLANDS COUNCIL
Council Offices, School Place,
Kirkwall KW15 1NY.
Telephone: Kirkwall (0856) 3535

SHETLAND ISLANDS COUNCIL
Town Hall, Lerwick,
Shetland ZE1 0HB.
Telephone: Lerwick (0595) 3535

WESTERN ISLES ISLANDS COUNCIL
Comhairle Nan Eilean,
Council Offices, Standwick Road,
Stornoway PA87 2BW.
Telephone: Stornoway (0851) 3773
Telex: 0851 3773

Northern Ireland

WATER SERVICE DIVISIONS

Eastern
1 College Square East, Belfast BT1
6DR.
Telephone: Belfast (0232) 328161

Northern
Thomas Street, Ballymena BT43 6BA.
Telephone: Ballymena (0266) 3655

Southern
Marlborough House, Central Way,
Craigavon BT64 1AD.
Telephone: Craigavon (0762) 41144

Western
P.O. Box 8, Altnagelvin,
Londonderry BT47 2LL.
Tel: Londonderry (0504) 46211

CALCIUM, CALORIES AND FAT CONTENT OF SOME POPULAR FAST FOODS

Kentucky Fried Chicken

Food	Calcium mg/svg	Calories per svg	Ca/Calorie Ratio	Fat (g) per svg	% Calories as Fat
Baked Beans (regular size)	63	90	0.70	1	10
Coleslaw (regular size)	38	125	0.30	9	65
Original Recipe Wing	38	181	0.21	12	60
Original Recipe Breast	48	276	0.17	17	55
Chicken Gravy	9	59	0.15	4	61
Original Recipe Centre Breast	39	257	0.15	14	49
Original Recipe Thigh	28	278	0.10	19	62
Kentucky Fries (regular size)	24	261	0.09	11	38
Original Recipe Drumstick	13	147	0.09	9	55
Corn on the Cob	7	134	0.05	3	20

McDonald's

Food	Calcium mg/svg	Calories per svg	Ca/Calorie Ratio	Fat (g) per svg	% Calories as Fat
Vanilla Milk Shake	329	352	0.93	8	20
Strawberry Milk Shake	322	362	0.89	9	22
Chocolate Milk Shake	320	383	0.84	9	21
Egg McMuffin	226	340	0.66	16	42
English Muffin with Butter	117	186	0.63	5	24
Cheeseburger	169	318	0.53	16	45

McDonald's – *continued*

Food	Calcium mg/svg	Calories per svg	Ca/Calorie Ratio	Fat (g) per svg	% Calories as Fat
Quarter Pounder with Cheese	255	525	0.49	32	55
Sausage McMuffin with Egg	196	517	0.38	33	57
Big Mac	203	570	0.36	35	55
Scrambled Eggs	61	180	0.34	13	65
Hamburger	84	263	0.32	11	38
Filet-O-Fish	133	435	0.31	26	54
Quarter Pounder	98	427	0.23	24	51
Hotcakes with Butter, Syrup	103	500	0.21	10	18
Apple Pie	14	253	0.06	14	50
French Fries	9	220	0.04	12	49
Apple Danish	14	389	0.04	18	42
Hashbrown Potatoes	5	144	0.03	9	56
Chicken McNuggets	11	323	0.03	20	56

Pizza Hut (UK) Ltd

	K Cal	% Calories as Fat	Calcium (mg)	Ca/ Calorie Ratio	Fat (g)
PIZZA – (SMALL – serves one)					
Sauce & Cheese Pizza (pan)	715	29.0	632	0.88	23
Sauce & Cheese Pizza (T & C)	458	59.0	459	1.00	30
Vegetarian (pan)	734	33.1	525	0.72	27
Vegetarian (T & C)	620	30.5	576	0.93	21
Spicy Hot One (pan)	780	34.6	551	0.71	30
Spicy Hot One (T & C)	722	37.4	531	0.74	30
Seafood Supreme (pan)	877	29.0	827	0.94	28
Seafood Supreme (T & C)	683	26.4	555	0.81	20
Supreme (pan)	830	40.0	566	0.68	37
Supreme (T & C)	643	41.0	685	1.07	29
Super Supreme (pan)	966	44.7	620	0.64	48
Super Supreme (T & C)	761	47.3	554	0.73	40

Pizza Hut (UK) Ltd – *continued*

	K Cal	% Calories as Fat	Calcium (mg)	Cal/ Calorie Ratio	Fat (g)
PASTA – (main course)					
Lasagne	529	40.8	325	0.61	24
Spaghetti bolognese	395	20.5	85	0.22	9
Tagliatelle Verdi Vegetarian	600	36.0	152	0.25	24
Tagliatelle Supreme	684	34.2	192	0.28	26
PRIAZZO – (SMALL – serves one to two people)					
Roma	989	45.5	667	0.67	50
Florentine	1,042	40.6	1,223	1.17	47
Verona	1,002	40.4	826	0.82	45
Mixed Regular Salad (no Dressing)	140	6.4	106	0.76	1
Mixed Regular Salad (with Dressing)	338	87.8	106	0.31	33

CALCIUM, CALORIES AND FAT CONTENT OF SOME POPULAR PREPARED FOODS

Findus Lean Cuisine

Dish	Weight (g)	Calories per svg	Calories per 100 g	Fat (g) per svg	Fat (g) per 100 g	% Calories as Fat	Calcium (mg) (% of RDA)	per svg (500 g)	Ca/Calorie Ratio
Zucchini Lasagne	312	256	82	6.9	2.2	24	60	300	1.17
Beef and Pork Cannelloni	273	235	86	8.2	3.0	31	46	230	0.98
Beef Provençale	269	269	100	12.9	4.8	43	31	155	0.58
Fillet of Cod with Broccoli	300	225	75	9	3.0	36	34	170	0.76
Spaghetti Bolognese	326	241	74	5.9	1.8	22	17	85	0.35
Kashmiri Chicken Curry	238	274	115	7.9	3.3	26	16	80	0.29
Lasagne Verdi with Broccoli, Chicken and Ham	275	261	95	7.7	2.8	27	16	80	0.31
Cheese Cannelloni	259	280	108	11.9	4.6	38	17	85	0.30
Turkey in Mushroom Sauce	290	194	67	5.5	1.9	26	12	60	0.31
Beef Italienne with Tagliatelle	250	235	94	6.3	2.5	24	10	50	0.21

Each dish = 1 serving.

ASDA Own Label Ready Meal Style Products

No data on calcium available. Typical values per 100 g (3.5 oz):

Product	Energy (kj)	Calories (kcal)	Protein (g)	Carbohydrate (g)	Fat (g)
Onion Bhaji	936	223	6.8	24.7	11.5
Lamb Samosa	1,183	283	6.8	25.1	18.0
Vegetable Samosa	1,002	240	3.9	25.2	14.4
Chicken Tikka	818	195	20.6	7.7	9.3
Chicken Spring Roll	755	180	6.2	22.1	8.0
Vegetable Spring Roll	748	178	4.8	26.1	7.0
Chicken Saté	972	232	30.2	4.4	10.5
Bacon Ribs in BBQ Sauce	446	170	7.0	2.5	7.8
Beef Stew with Dumplings	630	150	6.8	14.8	7.5
Lancashire Hotpot	447	100	7.4	9.0	4.8
Sausage & Mash	597	142	4.9	14.3	7.7
Crofter's Pie	550	131	6.1	12.4	6.7
Lasagne Verdi	609	145	6.1	15.4	7.0
Tagliatelle	507	121	4.3	13.5	5.9
Cannelloni	525	125	5.1	14.2	5.7
Cauliflower au Gratin	333	80	4.6	3.9	5.2
Vegetable Mornay	338	81	4.3	4.5	5.2
Potato Dauphinoise	592	142	2.8	11.8	9.6
Chicken Italienne	332	79	11.9	2.1	2.6
Chicken Supreme	732	174	9.6	14.9	8.9
Coronation Chicken	1,308	314	10.9	20.9	21.3
Chilli Con Carne	512	122	9.9	10.2	4.9

ASDA Own Label Ready Meal Style Products –
continued

Product	Energy (kj)	Calories (kcal)	Protein (g)	Carbohydrate (g)	Fat (g)
Cod Portions	320	75	17.5	Trace	0.6
Haddock Portions	316	75	17.5	Trace	0.5
Plaice Fillets	320	75	17.5	Trace	0.6
Whole Trout	554	132	10.5	Trace	6.0
Whole Prawns	342	81	17.0	1.0	1.0
Peeled Prawns	342	81	17.0	1.0	1.0
Smoked Cod	320	75	17.5	Trace	0.6
Smoked Haddock	316	75	17.5	Trace	0.5
Scottish Smoked Salmon	706	169	24.1	Trace	8.1
Cod in Bread Crumb	750	179	15.0	9.4	9.3
Haddock in Crumb	961	230	13.7	5.2	3.1
Plaice in Crumb	836	200	13.8	11.2	11.4
Scampi in Crumb	870	210	12.5	17.2	10.4
Haddock Goujons	808	193	15.0	12.8	9.4

OXALATES IN FOODS

Instructions: Milligrams of oxalates per 100 g (3.5 oz) serving are shown below. Oxalates bind calcium, making it unavailable. In predisposed individuals oxalates increase the risk of kidney stones. Individuals with a personal or family history of kidney stones should not consume more than 40 to 50 milligrams of oxalate per day.

Food	Oxalate (mg/100 g)
Spinach	750–1760
Rhubarb	860
Beetroot	675
Swiss chard	645
Wheat germ	270
Pecans	200
Peanuts	190
Parsley	165
Peppers, green and red	160
Okra	145
Chocolate	120
Lime peel	110
Leeks	90
Gooseberries	90
Lemon peel	85
Watercress	85
Tea, black – brewed 6 min	80
Tea, black – brewed 4 min	70
Tea, black – brewed 2 min	55
Tea, Darjeeling – brewed 1 min	25
Tea, green – brewed 3 min	35

Food	Oxalate (mg/100 g)
Sweet potatoes	55
Raspberries, black	55
Cabbage, Chinese	50
Celery	25–50
Beans, green	45
Aubergine	40
Hot cocoa (cup)	30
Carrots	6–30
Endive	30
Grapes, concord	25
Dandelion greens	25
Summer squash	20
Bread, whole wheat	20
Beans in tomato sauce	20
Currants, red	10–20
Swede	20
Blackberries	20
Blueberries	15
Raspberries, red	15
Strawberries	15
Cauliflower	1–15
Kale	7–15
Fruit salad	10
Plums	0–10
Marmalade	10
Tomatoes	2–10
Parsnips	10
Onions, green	10
Beansprouts (soy)	10
Strawberry jam	9
Artichokes	9
Cabbage	0–8
Mustard greens	8
Cake, sponge	7
Liver	7
Bread, white	7

Food	*Oxalate (mg/100 g)*
Apricots	3–7
Cranberry juice	7
Oranges	4–6
Brussels sprouts	0–6
Lettuce	2–6
Grape juice	6
Prunes	6
Asparagus	2–5
Corn	5
Potatoes, white (boiled)	0–5
Cornflakes	5
Fennel	5
Garlic	5
Peaches	1–5
Tomato juice	5
Vegetable soup	5
Sardines	2–5
Currants, black	4
Lima beans	4
Beer	0–4
Rosehip tea	4
Spaghetti in tomato sauce	4
Tofu	4
Bacon (fried)	3
Grapefruit	3
Coffee (brewed)	2–3
Kidney, braised	3
Wine (Beaujolais)	3
Apples	2–3
Pears	2–3
Tomato soup	3
Kohlrabi	3
Mushrooms	2
Pork (roast)	2
Beef (roast)	0–2
Ham	1–2

Food	Oxalate (mg/100 g)
Lamb (roast)	trace–2
Lemon juice	2
Pasta (boiled)	2
Pineapple (canned)	2
Wine (rosé)	2
Orange juice	1
Cherries	1
Chicken (roast)	1
Chives	1
Coffee, instant	1
Peas	1
Chicken noodle soup	1
Chow mein noodles	1
Cucumber	1
Oatmeal (cooked)	1
Oxtail soup	1
Turnips (boiled)	1
Banana	1
Milk	1
Plum jam, red	1
Pumpkin	1
Eggs (boiled)	1
Flounder (boiled)	1
Radishes	0–1
Beef, corned (canned)	0–1
Haddock	1
Apple juice	trace
Broccoli	trace
Coca-Cola	trace
Pepsi-Cola	trace
Sherry (dry)	trace
Wine (port)	trace
Avocado	0
Butter	0
Cantaloupe	0
Casaba melon	0

Food	Oxalate (mg/100 g)
Cheese, cheddar	0
Cider	0
Grapes, white	0
Grapefruit juice	0
Hamburger	0
Honeydew melon	0
Lime juice	0
Mangoes	0
Margarine	0
Nectarines	0
Onions, mature	0
Pineapple juice	0
Sweets, boiled	0
Rice (boiled)	0
Watermelon	0
Wine (white)	0

References

Ney, D. M. et al. *The Low Oxalate Diet Book for the Prevention of Oxalate Kidney Stones*. San Diego: University of California at San Diego Medical Center, 1981.

Yamanaka, H. et al. 'Determination of oxalate in foods by enzymatic analysis'. *Journal of the Food Hygiene Society of Japan* 1983; 24: 454–8.

Ohkawa, H. 'Gas chromatographic determination of oxalic acid in foods'. *Journal of the Association of Official Analytical Chemists* 1985; 68: 108–11.

Kim, E. H. and Im, K. J. 'A study of oxalic acid and calcium content in Korean foods'. *Korean Journal of Nutrition* 1977; 10: 292–8.

Hodgkinson, A. *Oxalic Acid in Biology and Medicine*. New York: Academic Press, 1977.

Morinaga Milk Co., Ltd., Tokyo, Japan. Personal communication.

Lentner, C., ed. *Geigy Scientific Tables*, 8th ed. West Caldwell, NJ: Medical Education Division, Ciba-Geigy Corp., 1981.

SOURCES OF POTASSIUM

Food (*100 g/3.5 oz portion, unless otherwise stated*)	Potassium (*mg*)
Prunes, raw	940
Raisins, raw	763
Banana (1)	740
Figs, dried	640
Nectarine (1)	588
Sole, baked	587
Scallops, steamed	476
Mushrooms, raw	414
Turkey breast, roasted	411
Chicken breast, roasted	411
Potato, boiled in skin	407
Peach (1)	404
Broccoli, raw	382
Tomato (1)	366
Salmon, canned sockeye	361
Celery, raw	341
Beetroot, raw	335
Milk, skimmed (8-oz glass)	334
Sardines, canned Pacific, drained	320
Clams, raw	311
Orange (1)	300
Plums, damson (3)	299
Cauliflower	295
Albacore tuna, raw	293
Apricot, raw	281
Asparagus, raw	278
Grapefruit ($\frac{1}{2}$)	270
Turnips, raw	268
Lettuce, butterhead	264

Food (*100 g/3.5 oz portion, unless otherwise stated*)	Potassium (mg)
Cabbage, raw	233
Corn on the cob	196
Grapes	173
Apple, raw (1)	165
Cucumber	160
Pineapple, raw	146
Ricotta	136
Shrimp, canned, drained	122
Swiss cheese	104
Cottage cheese	85
Blueberries, raw	81
Pasta	79

REFERENCES AND BIBLIOGRAPHY

Ackley, S., E. Barrett-Connor and L. Suarez. 'Dairy products, calcium, and blood pressure'. *American Journal of Clinical Nutrition* 38 (1983): 457–61.

Blot, W. J. et al. 'Geographic patterns of large bowel cancer in the United States'. *Journal of the National Cancer Institute* 57 (1976): 125–31.

—— 'Geographic patterns of breast cancer in the United States'. *Journal of the National Cancer Institute* 59 (1977): 1407–11.

Bouillon, R. A. et al. 'Vitamin D status in the elderly: seasonal substrate deficiency causes 1,25-dihydroxycholecalciferol deficiency'. *American Journal of Clinical Nutrition* 45 (1987): 755–63.

Buset, M. et al. 'Inhibition of human colonic epithelial cell proliferation in vivo and in vitro by calcium'. *Cancer Research* 46 (1986): 5426–30.

Canada, Minister of National Health and Welfare. *Mortality Atlas of Canada*. Hull, Quebec: Canadian Government Publishing Centre, 1980: Map 17.

Charlson, R. J. et al. 'The dominance of tropospheric sulfate in modifying solar radiation'. In *Radiation in the Atmosphere*, ed. H. J. Bolle. Princeton: Science Press, 1977: 32–38.

Colston, K., J. R. Wilkinson and R. C. Coombes. '1,25-dihydroxyvitamin D_3 binding in estrogen-responsive rat breast tumour'. *Endocrinology* 119 (1986): 397–403.

Cummings, S. R. et al. 'Epidemiology of osteoporosis and osteoporotic fractures'. *Epidemiologic Reviews* 7 (1985): 178–208.

Facchini, U. et al. 'Geographical variation of cancer mortality in Italy'. *International Journal of Epidemiology* 14 (1985): 538–48.

Finlayson-Pitts, B. J. and J. N. Pitts Jr. *Atmospheric Chemistry: Fundamentals and Experimental Techniques.* New York: John Wiley and Sons, 1986: 1098.

Gardner, M. J. et al. *Atlas of Cancer Mortality in England and Wales, 1968–1978.* Chichester, UK: John Wiley and Sons, 1983.

Garland, C. F. and F. C. Garland. 'Calcium and colon cancer'. *Clinical Nutrition* 5 (1986): 161–6.

—— 'Do sunlight and vitamin D reduce the likelihood of colon cancer?' *International Journal of Epidemiology* 9 (1980): 227–31.

Garn, S. M. and V. M. Hawthorne. 'Calcium intake and bone loss in population context'. In: *Calcium in Biological Systems,* ed. R. P. Rubin, G. B. Weiss, and J. W. Putney, Jr. New York: Plenum Press, 1985: 569–74.

Greenberg, M. R. *Urbanization and Cancer Mortality: The United States Experience, 1950–1975.* Monographs in epidemiology and biostatistics, volume 4. New York: Oxford University Press, 1983.

Grinstead, C. W., C. Y. C. Pak and G. J. Krejs. 'Effect of 1,25-dihydroxyvitamin D_3 on calcium absorption in the colon of healthy humans'. *American Journal of Physiology* 247 (1984): G189–92.

Hall, F. M., M. A. Davis and D. T. Baran. 'Bone mineral screening of osteoporosis'. *New England Journal of Medicine* 316 (1987): 212–14.

Haussler, M. R. 'Vitamin D receptors: nature and function'. *Annual Review of Nutrition* 6 (1986): 527–62.

Heaney, R. P. and R. R. Recker. 'Distribution of calcium absorption in middle-aged women'. *American Journal of Clinical Nutrition* 43 (1986): 299–305.

Hidy, G. M. *Aerosols.* New York: Academic Press, Inc., 1984.

Hodgkinson, A. *Oxalic Acid in Biology and Medicine*. New York: Academic Press, 1977.

Holick, M. F., J. A. MacLaughlin and S. H. Doppelt. 'Regulation of cutaneous previtamin D_3 photosynthesis in man: skin pigment is not an essential regulator'. *Science* 211 (1981): 590–93.

Karanja, N. and D. A. McCarron. 'Calcium and hypertension'. *Annual Review of Nutrition* 6 (1986): 475–94.

Kelsay, J. L. 'Effect of oxalic acid on calcium bioavailability'. In *Nutritional bioavailability of calcium*, ed. C. Kies. Based on a symposium sponsored by the Division of Agricultural and Food Chemistry at the 187th Meeting of the American Chemical Society, St Louis, Missouri 8–13 April 1984. ACS Symposium Series 275. Washington, DC: American Chemical Society, 1985, 105–16.

Kolonel, L. N. 'Fat and colon cancer: How firm is the epidemiologic evidence?' *American Journal of Clinical Nutrition* 45 (1987): 336–41.

Kondrat'ev, K. Y. A. *Radiation Characteristics of the Atmosphere and the Earth's Surface*. (Translated from the Russian.) New Delhi: Amerind Publishing Co., 1973.

Krueger, A. J. 'Sighting of El Chichon sulfur dioxide clouds with the Nimbus 7 total ozone mapping spectrometer'. *Science* 220 (1983): 1377–9.

Landsberg, H. E. et al. *World Maps of Climatology*. 2nd ed. New York: Springer-Verlag, 1965.

Lilienfeld, A. M. and D. E. Lilienfeld. *Foundations of Epidemiology*, 2nd ed. New York: Oxford University Press, 1980.

Lipkin, M. and J. H. Newmark. 'Effect of added dietary calcium on colonic epithelial-cell proliferation in subjects at high risk for familial colonic cancer'. *New England Journal of Medicine* 313 (1985): 1381–4.

London, J. 'The depletion of ultraviolet radiation by atmospheric ozone'. In *The Biologic Effects of Ultraviolet Radiation (with Emphasis on the Skin)*. Ed. F. Urbach. New York: Pergamon Press, 1969: 335–9.

McCance, R. A. and E. M. Widdowson. 'Mineral metabolism of healthy adults on white and brown bread dietaries'. *Journal of Physiology* 101 (London, 1942–43): 44.

McCarron, D. A. and C. D. Morris. 'Blood pressure response to oral calcium in persons with mild to moderate hypertension'. *Annals of Internal Medicine* 103 (1985): 825–31.

MacLaughlin, J. A., R. R. Anderson and M. F. Holick. 'Spectral character of sunlight modulates photosynthesis of previtamin D_3 and its photoisomers in human skin'. *Science* 216 (1982): 1001–3.

Martin, C. J. and W. J. Evans. 'Phytic acid–metal ion interactions. I. The effect of pH on CA(II) binding'. *Journal of Inorganic Biochemistry* 27 (1986): 17–30.

Mason, T. J. et al. *Atlas of Cancer Mortality for US Counties: 1950–69*. DHEW Publication No. (NIH)·75-780. Washington, DC: US Government Printing Office, 1975.

Matkovic, V. et al. 'Bone status and fracture rates in two regions of Yugoslavia'. *American Journal of Clinical Nutrition* 32 (1979): 540–49.

Miyaura, C. et al. '1,25-dihydroxyvitamin D_3 induces differentiation of human myeloid leukemia cells'. *Biochemical and Biophysical Research Communications* 102 (1981): 937–43.

Modan, B. et al. 'Low-fiber intake as an etiology factor in cancer of the colon'. *Journal of the National Cancer Institute* 55 (1975): 15–18.

Napalkov, N. P. et al. *Cancer Incidence in the USSR*. Supplement to *Cancer Incidence in Five Continents*, Volume 3. IARC Scientific Publication No. 48. Lyon: International Agency for Research on Cancer, 1983: 59.

Newmark, H. L., M. J. Wargovich and W. R. Bruce.

'Colon cancer and dietary fat, phosphate, and calcium: A hypothesis'. *Journal of the National Cancer Institute* 72 (1984): 1323–5.

Ney, D. M. et al. *The Low Oxalate Diet Book for the Prevention of Oxalate Kidney Stones.* San Diego: General Clinical Research Centre, University of California, San Diego, 1981.

Palm, T. A. 'The geographical distribution and aetiology of rickets'. *The Practitioner* 45 (1890): 270–79.

Pennington, J. A. T. and H. N. Church. *Bowes and Church's Food Values of Portions Commonly Used*, 14th ed. Philadelphia: J. B. Lippincott Co., 1985.

Petrakis, N. L., V. L. Ernster and M.-C. King. 'Breast'. In *Cancer Epidemiology and Prevention*, ed. D. Schottenfeld and J. F. Fraumeni Jr. Philadelphia: W. B. Saunders Company, 1982: 855–70.

Phillips, R. L. and D. A. Snowdon. 'Dietary relationships with fatal colorectal cancer among Seventh-Day Adventists'. *Journal of the National Cancer Institute* 74 (1985): 307–17.

Potter, J. D. and A. J. McMichael. 'Diet and cancer of the colon and rectum: A case-control study'. *Journal of the National Cancer Institute* 76 (1986): 557–69.

Recker, R. R. and R. P. Heaney. 'The effect of milk supplements on calcium metabolism, bone metabolism, and calcium balance'. *American Journal of Clinical Nutrition* 41 (1985): 254–63.

Schottenfeld, D. and S. J. Winawer. 'Large intestine'. In *Cancer Epidemiology and Prevention*, ed. D. Schottenfeld and J. F. Fraumeni Jr. Philadelphia: W. B. Saunders Company, 1982: 703–27.

Scotto, J., T. E. Fears and J. F. Fraumeni Jr. 'Solar radiation'. In *Cancer Epidemiology and Prevention*, ed. D. Schottenfeld and J. F. Fraumeni Jr. Philadelphia: W. B. Saunders Company, 1982: 254–76.

Scotto, J., T. R. Fears and G. B. Gorio. 'Ultraviolet exposure patterns, 1976'. *Environmental Research* 12 (1976): 228–37.

Seidman, H. and S. D. Stellman. 'A different perspective on breast cancer risk: Some implications of the non-attributable risk'. *Cancer* 32 (1982): 301–13.

Shekelle, R. B. et al. 'Dietary vitamin A and risk of cancer in the Western Electric Study'. *Lancet* 2 (1981): 1185–90.

Shimkin, M. B. *Science and Cancer*, 3rd rev. Washington, DC: US Department of Health and Human Services, National Cancer Institute, 1980.

Smith, L. H. 'The diagnosis and treatment of metabolic stone disease'. *Medical Clinics of North America* 56 (1972): 977–88.

Solomons, N. W. 'Calcium intake and availability from the human diet'. *Clinical Nutrition* 5 (1986): 167–76.

Sowers, M. R. et al. 'The association of intakes of vitamin D and calcium with blood pressure among women'. *American Journal of Clinical Nutrition* 42 (1985): 135–42.

Waggoner, A. P. et al. 'Optical characteristics of atmospheric aerosols'. *Atmospheric Environment* 15 (1981): 1891–1909.

Wargovich, M. J., V. W. Eng and H. L. Newmark. 'Calcium inhibits the damaging and compensatory proliferative effects of fatty acids on mouse colon epithelium'. *Cancer Letters* 23 (1984): 253–8.

Warshauer, M. C. et al. 'Stomach and colorectal cancers in Puerto Rican-born residents of New York City'. *Journal of the National Cancer Institute* 75 (1986): 592–5.

Willett, W. C. et al. 'Dietary fat and the risk of breast cancer'. *New England Journal of Medicine* 316 (1987): 22–8.

INDEX

Page references in *italics* indicate
tables or figures.